To Have or Not To Have That is the Question

The Economics of Desire

Nilton Bonder

*Our mission is to efficiently provide the world's finest, most comprehensive book publishing
service, enabling every author to experience success. To find out how to publish your book, your
way, and have it available worldwide, visit us online at www.trafford.com*

Trafford rev. 05/14/2010

 www.trafford.com

North America & international
toll-free: 1 888 232 4444 (USA & Canada)
phone: 250 383 6864 ♦ fax: 812 355 4082

To:

Dório, Sima, Marcelo, Clarissa,
Bruno and Marianna
Ferman

Translated by Diane Grosklaus Whitty

Table of Contents

Chapter IV
Spiritual Realm
To Have or Not to Have? — That is the teiku *(paradox)!*

Chapter V
The Economics of Desire

Introduction

Having is fundamental, essential, and indispensable.

Submerged in a world of consumerism and materialism, we are perplexed by what has happened to us. How did we end up building this world? Where does this reality of ours come from?

It is a world where power is measured by our ability to buy, where entertainment and celebrations take place in shopping malls, where dreams are fulfilled through consumption, and where feelings and trends take their cues from the market. How did our world get to be like this?

I'm one of those people who doesn't believe things are the result of ignorance. I think we blame ignorance so we don't have to cope with other kinds of 'intelligences'. Whether it is positive or negative, constructive or destructive, there is a logic, or truth, that pervades our reality.

This book tries to lay bare the role of possession—better put, the indispensability of possession. In it, possession is not seen as anything pathological. By definition, existence itself means possessing a body. Being is having, and this being begins with an act of possession. Our life choices will always take the form of acts of possession, but true possession is shaped not only by what we have but also, and just as importantly, by what we do not have. This is the ongoing dilemma of possession: what to have and what not to have!

Our existence finds expression in the things we have but also in the things we don't have—in the things we'd like to possess and the things we deliberately decide not to have.

Our being and our history are always trajectories of possession: that is, of the things we possess and do not possess, of the people we possess and do not possess, of what we make our fate and what we don't make our fate. Living means deciding between having or not having things, others, and our selves.

No problem lies in the essence of "having"; the problem comes when there is no dilemma between having and not having. If possession is only a one-way street—that is, if we have and hold things for ourselves and monopolize what is dispensable to being—then possession has a disastrous impact on our existence. Having is never dispensable. Having can never be a mental or abstract state dissociated from a tangible need. When it is, then do our misfortunes begin, for whenever being and having are not flip sides of the same coin, they become the antithesis of each other.

Precisely because we are mortal, finite, and exhaustible, we experience the feeling of existence. Yet these characteristics are not limitations on our existence; rather, they express its very essence. "Being" means needing "to have," which in turn means that "having" must adjust to the boundaries of "being." When "having" is fitting and fair, it dissolves into the experience of "being."

When abstract "having" comes to us even before we have a real need, we end up evading our fundamental and inescapable task of deliberating about whether "to have or not have," and this proves disastrous for us.

Whenever "having" is rooted in need, however, it is a tool and a source of nourishment for "being"—in other words, it will reinforce the measures and boundaries that shape our experience of "being." Whenever "having" appropriates something outside the real limits of "being," that is, something unjustified by any true need for it, we will lose tonus and our experience of "being" will become flaccid.

"Having" is, and always will be, the essential question of existence. "Being" is, and always will be, a question of matter.

These reflections explore the tangled human experiences and phenomena that have made our relationship with possession so complex—better put, that have made it a "question."

Interchangeability in Shakespeare

Every formula is a reduction to the simplest terms. It's the ultimate synthesis of relations in life or nature. "To be or not to be? That is the question!" defines a relationship between decision-making and motivation. Choosing "to be" or "not to be" is life's object of interest.

Let's assume that being and having are interchangeable and can be mistaken for each other, so long as we understand having as a measure between what we have and what we deliberately don't have. If having is the choice that emerges from the real demand of the moment, and not an imperative of our imagination or a mental construct, then this formula permits the interchangeability of having and being. This interchangeability is the central issue of this book. But before delving into it, we must establish an important definition: what is a "question"?

The word "question" can be understood in a number of ways, a fact that became quite evident when Shakespeare was translated into Yiddish. Originating as a German dialect used by some Jews, Yiddish has become the lingua franca of the exiled Jew. I don't know of any similar phenomenon among other peoples, where a group has adopted as its national language a dialect that is a testament to its exile—a mother tongue that is actually a stepmother tongue. It is a language that expresses being (identity) in the absence of having (territory)—or even better put, being as a function of not having.

The translator who rendered *Hamlet* into Yiddish couldn't decide how to handle the word "question." Beyond the apparently philosophical heart of this Shakespearian formula, Yiddish highlights another of the equation's unknowns, namely "that's the question." What precisely is meant by the word "question," which in Yiddish can be translated in different ways, as *frague*, (query), *shaila* (ambivalence), *kashia* (doubt), or *teiku* (paradox)?

These four nearly synonymous words reflect subtle distinctions that the Yiddish culture has perceived within the realms of human inquiry. This may be a result of its roots in German, a language characterized by exceedingly accurate usage of words for every specific situation. Or it may simply be a product of the Yiddish culture's intra-psychological characteristics. We know from jokes and anecdotes that the tradition of "questioning" is one of its cultural traits. The fact is, Yiddish offers us a gamut of nuanced variations for the word "question."

The first possible translation of "query" refers to a straightforward search for unavailable information. Our need for answers is essential to survival itself; it involves a concrete search rooted in questions about our physical world. If I don't know, I'll pose a query; I'll ask. That's how many people read Shakespeare; in other words, this is what we should be asking ourselves, period.

The second translation—"ambivalence"— underscores emotional aspects of our questioning. In Yiddish, a *shaila* was what a disciple would ask a sage whenever some new realization aroused a disturbing perplexity or ambiguity in him. Any new insight affects a number of areas in our lives, and we're not always ready and willing to accept this interference. "But if this is like this…then shouldn't that be like that?"—this is what someone with a *shaila* really wants to know. His conclusion influences other areas of his life, and this confuses him. Entrenched worldviews clash with a new idea. The focus of such questions lies within the emotional realm.

The third translation for "question"—"doubt"— entails the intellectual realm. In Yiddish, *kashia* are what the sages themselves asked about the precision or accuracy of an aphorism. Imprecise concepts cannot serve as corollaries of other concepts. Thought demands consistent ideas if it is not to be lost in illusions. A *kashia* looks not only for an idea's intrinsic coherence but also for all possible implications regarding other ideas; without such consistency, a whole structure for comprehending reality would be jeopardized.

The fourth translation—"paradox"—refers to the spiritual dimension. The word *"teiku"* is an anagram formed from the first letters of the sentence "The prophet Elias will explain this *kashia*" in Hebrew. When the Talmudic sages could not reach a conclusion, or when the incongruence or contradiction between possible truths surpassed their ability to exhaust a question, such questions would remain open until some future time. It was rather like temporarily renouncing the attempt to reconcile two apparently contradictory truths. The prophet Elias symbolized a future of revelations and answers that we can only perceive as incongruities today. Until the future comes, the incoherence of such ideas does not render them invalid; they remain in a state of tension, part of a logical relation that is only acceptable based on intuition or convictions which cannot be proven.

These four dimensions reflect four different worlds—physical, emotional, intellectual, and spiritual—each associated with a possible interpretation of the word "question." These four worlds in turn correspond to a time-honored interpretive method the Kabbalists used to help them understand reality. By breaking reality down into these different levels, they could observe it more acutely and with greater clarity upon reassembling it.

We are going to use the same tool to subdivide Shakespeare's formula into four realms. Instead of "To be or not to be," we will ask the question "To have or not to have," and instead of using the common word "question," we will use four ways of interpreting the term: a query within the physical realm, an ambivalence within the emotional realm, a doubt within the intellectual realm, and a paradox within the spiritual realm.

So we will explore different ways of approaching the question:

1) To Have or Not to Have? — that is the *frague* (query)!

2) To Have or Not to Have? — that is the *shaila* (ambivalence)!

3) To Have or Not to Have? — that is the *kashia* (doubt)!

4) To Have or Not to Have? — that is the *teiku* (paradox)!

Being and Having

Our task in this book will be to weave a web between these two verbs. Our childhood is marked by efforts to distinguish between the two—not an easy task at all. The glance of a newborn baby, who feels he and his mother are one and the same being, and the issues of separation that this child will later face, intimate the linguistic and conceptual complexity of differentiating between being and having.

This challenge is what makes children voracious consumers by nature. Knowing this, the toy industry spends a fortune on ads that appeal to the childhood feeling that having a toy is vital to the child's being. Even when a toddler has grown more mature, and education and experience have taught him to distinguish somewhat between the two verbs, the question persists. Let's take as an example the way parents (or the world) display fairness towards two or more siblings. We might say that what these siblings have and how they perceive the attention and help they receive will determine categorically how they see themselves. Jealousy and envy continuously confound being with having.

The ability to distinguish between these two verbs is evidently so essential to human development that they are not conflated in any tongue. While many languages—like English—fuse the conceptually distinct Portuguese and Spanish verbs *ser* ("to be" in a permanent sense: "I am from Brazil") and *estar* ("to be" in a temporary sense: "I am in Brazil"), the same is not true of the verbs "to have" and "to be." There is no language in which the first is not conceptually distinct from the second. The web we will try to weave between these two verbs has nothing to do with a regression to infantile stages when the two are confused; rather, it recognizes the act of being as continually defined by values that guide our choice to have or not to have. It is this choice that separates childhood experience from mature experience. Perhaps rather than saying that being and having are interchangeable, it would be more accurate to say that being is absolutely interchangeable with having or not having.

Mystics from a wide range of traditions have realized that herein lies the greatest source of confusion and suffering for human beings. Even Karl Marx tried to establish a relation between possession and existence, when he asked whether man's consciousness determined his being or, to the contrary, if his being determined his consciousness. By "consciousness" I mean that which we have and which is objectified in our waking state. Psychoanalysis has defined consciousness as the dynamic relationship between what we have and what we deliberately don't have (subconscious). This mental-emotional "to have or not to have," which largely defines the experience of being, is responsible for our memory and our sense of self. There is a profound correlation between our perception of our Ego and our perception of an object—the perception of what I have and the perception of what the world have.

For the mystics, however, being did not determine consciousness nor did consciousness determine being; this depended on the mutual relationship between the two.

Being is the act of valuing things, people, or projects and transforming them into demands made by the entity we are and we administrate. For a human being, these values can be physical, emotional, intellectual, or spiritual. These are the terms under which being determines the reality around it—somewhat akin to how modern science discovers that the presence of a body interferes with the physics of a space. For the mystics, reality can be broken down into physical, emotional, intellectual, and spiritual components, because these are the tools of human perception. And what we perceive determines what we are. We perceive ourselves in these four realms because we are equipped with sensitive systems that allow us to feel present in these dimensions. If we had different senses, we would be different.

Our sense of being comes into existence as a function of the world around us. And the world around us is better known to us by what we have and what we don't have. Being is built out of the values it defines, and what we perceive as memory is nothing more than a triggering of our successful or failed efforts to honor these values. It is no mere coincidence that when we talk about the "value" of things we can have, we use the same word as when we talk about the "values" that guide our existence, in the name of which we are even capable of forfeiting that existence. When we die in the name of an ideal, we are "being" in the quest to be true to an important value. We so intensely want "to have" something accomplished that we are capable of jeopardizing the whole of our being.

Middle Eastern fundamentalism and its human-bombs scorn Western fear, which is incapable of making the supreme act of "consumption"—converting its "being" in the ultimate project of "having." Disguised as humanism, this Western incapacity is a form of attachment and fixation that turns life into a fetish. This is not to condone in any way the acts of violence and bloodshed that have been so manipulated in our times, but to acknowledge how this poses profound questions to our civilization. Without values, "being" cannot be sustained. We are not something that exists *per se*; we are a function of the values we assign to the entire gamut of possibilities that our senses may know. In this sense, religion is the maximization of these "values," because it projects them not just as the wishes and demands of an individual but as the absolute wish and supreme demand, whose subject is not I but God.

Understanding values is essential to understanding being, while it also delineates the boundaries of having and not having. We only value what we can have by making a holy decision about what we will not have.

Value and Values

Existence is a function not only of our body's demands but of our ability to tailor these demands to what is available in the world outside us. If a monkey's desire for a banana were absolute, then the monkey would see the value of the banana as absolute or paramount. But its yen for a banana can be satisfied by other kinds of food. What reality offers us will be determinant in our choice to have or not have because one of the definitions of "value" is how much work or effort is needed to realize our desire. The amount of sacrifice, that is, how much a demand forces us to give up, determines its value—or what we want to have or don't want to have.

If I have to pay too high a price to satisfy my demand, it is something I don't want to have. This cost means my initial desire to have is better represented by a decision to not have. In other words, value is an ongoing comparison between what we don't want to have and what our original drive (detached from the outer world) wanted us to try to have. Value is the relationship between having and not having that positions a person on the boundary between his inner and outer worlds. For a human being, it therefore requires the economic administration of one's self in the broadest sense, expressed in cost/benefit ratios within all four realms of our perception.

The same kind of criteria that determine values in our physical world—utility and scarcity—can also be found in our emotional, intellectual, and spiritual worlds. We endeavor to assign a precise figure to the purely subjective, relational values of having or not having in all four of these realms, as we will see later. It is not only physical want that lends worldly "things" value but emotional, intellectual, and spiritual wants as well. The priorities and limitations of existence have a major impact on our decisions about what to have or not have. The quality of our experience of being is reflected in the depth and precision of these valuations.

When his life comes to a close, who is it that finds himself feeling he has best accomplished the task of managing his life? He who was best able to define values and who therefore put greater effort into having certain things and into not having others.

But it is not only in the final accounting of our lives that these values determine the success of our endeavors, or lack thereof. Our very wellbeing is intricately dependent on how adroitly we manage this relationship between our values and the world around us. The correlation between wellbeing and honesty is of the tightest kind. Only if you are honest during the day will you sleep well at night. This honesty has nothing to do with moral honesty but with honesty about our values—the relationships that our being establishes in the midst of its environment.

Spiritual traditions tend to frame these choices between values or immediate satisfaction as the great existential "temptation" (that is, question). Jewish tradition has its own terms for this issue: the Evil Impulse and the Good Impulse. The term "evil" applies to situations in which we satisfy an immediate demand while sacrificing greater demands that generally entail medium- or long-term rewards. Whenever we make a choice to have which is not tied to any value, we are responding to an Evil Impulse. We will pay a price for this impulse, the highest of which is the absence of wellbeing. It must be stressed that evil is not an absolute characterization but a gauge of the relationship between being and having. The origin of every Evil Impulse is necessity itself (that is, limitations or wants), which is the fuel of existence.

Unless we have demands, there is no place for us in existence. Having all our needs met at the moment our desire blooms is the very definition of death. More than anything else, death represents the end of an entity's need to participate in exchanges with its environment. Physical matter will continue to engage in such exchanges, but death terminates the organic status that generated demands in order to preserve its organized project. Since there are no more chances of having, being is no longer possible. The Evil Impulse is the sacred lifeblood of immediate needs felt by an organism. There is no way to exist without the Evil Impulse, which in itself bespeaks the depth of this term. The Evil Impulse reflects the relational aspect of existence because what is most essential to its construction contains the very element that may destroy it. But it couldn't be any other way in a process aimed at achieving balance. A venom can always serve as an antidote, just as medicine can act as a poison. When it comes to attaining a balance, both want and excess are equally toxic.

The Good Impulse, on the other hand, is a product of culture. The word "culture" brings to mind a system outside us that subjects us to rules and directives. Yet this system is a product of the human experience of existence itself. We could say that every individual constructs his small individual culture through his process of experience and his history of existence in the world. When we experiment with our relationship to the world through the Evil Impulse, we begin to understand how it is—or isn't—good at promoting life. Our collective culture and personal experience help reshape the Evil Impulse into a Good Impulse, with the sole purpose of increasing our efficacy in the world and our wellbeing. Value is about refining an Evil Impulse into a Good Impulse.

There are no Good Impulses per se. Instead, these are always Evil Impulses reworked by value. Indeed, there is actually no "good" per se. Whatever can be "a good" (something good for existence) is by nature something we can "have" if we take value as our guide. Without value, there is no "good." Our "goods" will always be Evil Impulses that were reshaped into good. Without this process of refinement, the Evil Impulse will produce "evils," and sooner or later we will have to pay the price.

Life is therefore a management process. There is room not just for acts of survival – for living on – but also for strategies for living out a life as full as it can be, including its continuity into new generations. Wellbeing is generated by these three components – survival, wholeness (peace) and continuity – and cannot be achieved without the intermediation of values.

The stages of possession

There's a Yiddish saying that we are born with our hand closed and die with our hand open. The process of life begins with extreme attachment and should end with minimal attachment. The physical experience of life is inarguably about having a body. And our commitment to this body is to protect and care for it so we do not lose it. Having our self is life's greatest value.

But this value decreases over time.

If I have a ten-year lease on a business and I pay for its goodwill, the value of this goodwill falls over time. When the lease is about to expire, it is worthless. The same happens with possession of our bodies. In our youth, our bodies are priceless because they are at their greatest potential. Even objects, which a child very often sees as extensions of his own self, are assigned an astronomic value. We often laugh at a child who throws a fit because he doesn't get the object he wants. His grief is as deep as that of a person who has lost his dearest loved one. The child will only find consolation the same way this bereaved adult does, that is, when life offers a new set of possibilities that make him forget the experienced loss.

This child actually teaches us that the subjective value of an object can only be objectified when exchanged for another object. In our early years, such objects are of course other objects, or other physical things, which can mediate the loss. We can only imagine not having something if we get something else. Not having means getting a replacement for what we wanted to have. Anything else is intolerable.

A child intuitively begins to value things based on their utility as well as their scarcity. What do you want for your birthday? Clothes or a toy? For most children, a toy is what's useful, since it's more attractive to them. If there are only a few vacant swings in a park, while all the other playground equipment is unoccupied, it's not surprising that fighting and crying break out, because the children all want the same thing—whatever is scarce. Just as in the world of adult values, rarity is a parameter for possession and its values.

Our conceptions of value develop as we grow and our intelligence learns to recognize the parameters of value. How much work will be involved if I don't do this? What will it cost me in terms of time, bother, or loss if I do this or don't do that? Such configurations quickly take shape in our heads and at some point our brain becomes an organ that discerns values. All intelligence is about formulating values. The more abstract and complex a person's ability to understand cost/benefits in the short, medium, or long run—that is, to understand values—the smarter and more efficient he will be.

According to *Ethics of the Fathers*, there are four types among men: [1]

He who says, "What is yours is mine, and what is mine is mine"—he is a wicked man.

He who says, "What is mine is mine and what is yours is yours"—this is the common type, though some say that this is the type of Sodom.

He who says, "What is mine is yours and what is yours is mine"—philosopher (an unaware man). [2]

And he who says, "What is mine is yours and what is yours is thine own"—he is a saintly man.

---

1   *Pirkei Avot* (*Ethics of the Fathers*): Tractate of the Mishna that compiles the teachings of the rabbis and masters, written some two thousand years ago.

2   *Am ha-arets – literally means one who is not well educated or is an ill-informed individual. It also conveys the negative connotation of "rude" and "boorish." I have chosen to translate it as "philosopher" because in the past, rational and more down-to-earth individuals were portrayed as possessing great knowledge and capacity, even though incapable of achieving the deepest understandings, believed attainable only by men of faith.

I would venture to argue that these are not four different individuals but four stages of human development within one same individual. We start out in the physical dimension, where we acquire all our physical attributes. We master the use of our limbs, our coordination, and even our minds in their physical sense. We learn how to remember and store helpful information. We grow into our maximum physical form between childhood and puberty. This is our physical period, which culminates with the maturation of our sexual organs, making our sense of plenitude dependent not only on mastery over our own body but also on our ability to perpetuate this body through reproduction. During this stage, the chief characteristic of possession is having things.

The second moment in human development is the emotional stage, where love is the predominant element. Translating love received into love offered and shifting from paternal and maternal coordinates to the coordinates of a spouse or lover summarizes the essence of this moment. Possession will display its own unique characteristics during this phase. If the apex of our physical stage is the blossoming of a penis or vagina-uterus, the emotional stage culminates with the discovery of a heart that loves and is able to assume the commitments vital to the loving phase of conceiving, generating, and caring for our continuity. As an apprentice of paternity or maternity, a lover lives and takes his nourishment from the heart. In this stage, the prime feature of possession is "having" other people.

The third stage of development is mental. Up until this point, life had found expression in the physical realm that defined the body (the text of existence) and soon after in the emotional realm that defined its bonds (the context of existence). Human maturation next leads to the world of symbols and abstract meaning. The intellectual, or philosophical, world represents a stage where neither physical virility nor emotional vitality can respond to the values of the stage and where possession gains its own peculiar form. During this phase, the relevant values are focused not so much on the body we have but on a body we will not have. Here, the fundamental aspect of possession is having the uniqueness to make a difference. It is the feeling that our lives have a meaning.

In the fourth and final stage, spiritual values hold sway. These values are the boundaries of a body we will not have. The utility and scarcity that shape values during other stages of life will display fewer physical, emotional, and philosophical characteristics in this one. No longer defined by "what is worth it," these values are a mystifying contrast with all other stages, when value was determined through comparative estimates with other things or objects. In this final stage, possession is characterized by what we don't have.

Each of these stages has a specific relation to the basic question: "To Have or Not to Have." We are now going to explore the different "questions" related to having or not having, stage by stage.

Chapter I

Physical Realm

To Have or Not to Have? — That is the
frague (query)!

WHAT'S MINE IS MINE — WHAT'S YOURS IS MINE

We begin our lives asking ourselves very clear questions about our own limits. Who am I? Where do I begin and where do I end? Birth is inarguably the moment of our individualization. Until parturition, which parts us from a whole other being, we are unaware of the need to define our self. This is a period when our brain achieves amazing feats of self-adjustment. In order for us to see, our brain will have to interpret images received by our eyes and organize them according to distinguishable patterns. Our hearing will also be constructed, taking stimuli from our eardrums and learning to interpret certain configurations and patterns that will help us decipher the external world's sound structure.

These interpretations are processed by our senses and gain form during the first stages of life, and they will accompany us for the rest of our lives.

Yet among all the tasks required to format life, the most complex is our task of developing a sense of self, a boundary for our self, and a clear-cut representation of our body and individuality under our brain's management. Just as light teaches us to see, and sounds to hear, it is having and not having that teaches our brain about our size in the world.

Defined during our childhood, this size will be with us for the rest of our lives. We can optimize certain aspects of "our size" through in-depth therapy that readjusts the way we see ourselves, but it will be very hard to actually redimension the size of our self as it was configured during our first dealings with the world around us.

Within the physical dimension, or in the first stage of our lives, competitiveness is crucial and there is no greater value than "what's mine is mine and what's yours is mine." We generally think this attitude is inappropriate and socially unacceptable, but during this stage it is the only possible moral attitude that has value.

Children who are thwarted in their quest to "have" may become seriously maladjusted and envious of what they will always view as unclaimed possessions.

This is a time of utter fascination with and attraction to our Evil Impulse. This impulse that makes us want things is vital to our survival, and it cannot be replaced. This is the only moment when our immediate desire and our values are one and the same. When we satisfy our body's demands, we are learning about how to be, and this knowledge will last us a lifetime. Grab everything within your reach with the close-fisted hand of your birth. This is the only way to know the world around you, the world that will teach you that there are some things you don't want to have. It is up to the world, and not to morality, to teach you what you want to have and what you don't want to have. When a little friend who doesn't want to share his sucker gives you a hard shove, you will learn there are limits to wanting to have. These limits emanate from the very limits of our being and will be vital in constructing our experience of being.

It is during this stage that we come to know the meaning of possession. Possession exists. Contrary to how morality portrays it, possession is not something we can't take with us from this world. In fact, the only thing we will take with us to our grave is this possession that reveals our size to us in the first stage of our lives. And whoever fails to probe deep into the limits of what he would like to have will spend his whole life burdened by fantasies of seizing unclaimed possessions. These are the kleptomaniacs (in the closet or not) who will always want to take something for themselves but won't understand where their compulsion comes from. It has to do with sizes that were not consummated and with aspects of our view of our own physical body that never came sharply into focus for us. These are pathologies of being and the source of dysfunctions in our faculty of having.

Spoiling and abusing are both examples of such dysfunctions. A child spoiled by his parents is deprived of the experience of knowing his own size; his relation to possession will seem to emanate from a universal right to be a "little darling." He will not have a chance to experience "what's mine is mine and what's yours is mine." Instead, he will only know the concept of "what is is mine." The limits of the other and the concept of "yours" will be distorted, consequently distorting this child's knowledge of his own size. His Evil Impulse will be exaggerated, born out of imbalance, because his parents' exaggerated, immediate satisfaction of his desires hampered the child's construction of values towards the world.

On the other hand, the child who suffers any type of abuse, or of violent impediments that keep him from having, does not know "what's mine is mine," and the only size of self he will develop will involve "what's yours is mine." It's not enough to take the other child's lollipop away in order to learn your own size; we must also know that there are lollipops meant just for us, besides the ones we can grab away from our little friends. Nature offers a certain measure of care and concern, which leaves us with the feeling that we are truly deserving; without this, our chances to possess and our experience of being are at risk.

Complete possession is not an obsession, but rather a relational state that precludes the latter deviation. Playing with your toy car or your doll, while refusing to share with anyone else, is a magical experience that helps define the limits of our existence. Who doesn't have some amazing memory of this kind of experience, when a gift summed up our deepest sense of being, of determining our power and size? In many ways the final goal of possessing is to possess one's self.

However, it will be our defeats—the yours that do not become mine—that initiate us into values. We'd like the world to be free of costs, offering nothing but benefits. But life belongs to another realm, the realm of values established in the course of exchanges and interactions. Life means there will always be "mine" and there will always be "yours." The merger of yours into mine does not determine size, and there is no body without size. Size is as far as I can be, as far as the external world will let me be.

Herein lies the greatest potential of the physical dimension: occupying and making things available for the self. Everything beautiful in the physical realm is made to be possessed. Muscularity, dexterity, agility, and everything else that can make the physical beautiful involves our skills in having and getting. The physical being is a direct function of "having." Expecting any other kind of manifestation from the physical world is tantamount to not understanding it.

The overriding question of our physical world is a *frague*—a query. It is the simple gathering of information about what is mine and what can become mine. These queries are posed within the universe where we learn about using things and people. By taking possession of objects and people, we are able to enjoy benefits and pleasures, but these pleasures are limited by what determines value. They are limited externally by competitiveness and internally by the dynamics and idiosyncrasies of the gratification we derive from possession and ownership.

In the external realm, queries are ways of collecting information about how far we can go when we take for ourselves. How much will the outer world let me appropriate and, if it doesn't let me, how much will I be able to accomplish by relying on my greatest ally: the Evil Impulse, or my desire of the moment. Our first values will be brutally built through experiences such as our inability to take the lollipop away from our childhood friend. The query par excellence is: How can we navigate impossibilities and negotiate with this outer world as best we can?

In the inner realm, queries are inquiries about pleasure itself. Possession also allows us to get to know the very characteristics of being. We don't know how much pleasure we can gain from objects or even people, and this line of inquiry will tell us things about being. So we discover that we need variety and change as much as familiarity. Things bore and tire us over time, and we find gratification in novelty. The toy we possess affords us a fleeting sense of wellbeing, which quickly diminishes in value as we grow used to it. On the other hand, there are familiar things, like the teddy bear we sleep with—our "transitional" objects—whose value is derived precisely from their constancy and permanence. In terms of the physical world, people are objects—love objects, security objects. The same laws about familiarity and novelty apply to them. This is why people think children are capable of such cruelty, like someone who resorts to his Evil Impulse in an attempt to maximize his self. This is neither a good nor an evil process; it is merely an attempt to accomplish the task of being.

Thus it is important to understand what a *frague*—a query—is. To be in this world means mostly the task of configuring our organism to cope with external and internal instabilities. In its dynamic workings, our brain commissions the body and sends it off on a remarkable quest to seek out information. These are the questions: How do I work? How does the world work? How do I coordinate these different functions?

A *frague* is the product of an intelligence that is not just cerebral but organic and existential. Everything that behaves like a structure, like a life, is equipped with this intelligence that is capable of adjusting and adapting outer and inner instabilities. Since we only seem to need things and the world seems to be made up of things, we tackle the difficult task of testing the world out and assigning it values.

Without these *fragues*, without these queries, I cannot be. And these *fragues* are all processed through questions about what I can have and what I can't have. We must understand that when they come in the form of queries, our questions about being have to do with our human installation, or initial configuration. The organic intelligence implicit to our very structure allows us to install ourselves in the world, while trying to optimize ourselves. Through this process, we come to know ourselves and to experience being.

Chapter II

Emotional Realm

To Have or Not to Have? — That is the
shaila (ambivalence)!

WHAT'S MINE IS MINE — WHAT'S YOURS IS YOURS

In this realm, the emotional aspect is at the fore. Of course, emotional aspects are present in all phases of life, notably in childhood, when their profound conditioning marks us for the whole of our existence. But while on the one hand expressions of the four worlds—physical, emotional, intellectual, and spiritual—are always present in our lives, during certain phases some of them play the leading roles in our interactions with the world.

9

During this specific period of our lives, changes in our body and the maturation of our organism will alter our relations to things and also to whatever we want to obtain and gain possession of. Puberty and the attainment of sexual maturity represent this new bodily stage, which inaugurates a new relation with what we want to have and what we don't want to have. Bodily changes always announce the beginning of a new stage; the body is the foundation upon which we build all our faculties and life experiences.

Precisely because of these changes in our bodies, a new kind of question emerges: *shailas*, or ambivalences. Our wants will gradually be modified and the features of possession will differ from the previous phase. We can better understand the characteristics of this new phase, where the focus is on emotional activity, if we borrow a parable from Reb Nachman of Breslov: [3]

Because once upon a time a king so desired a princess, he worked hard and plotted to seduce her, until he eventually succeeded. And she stayed with him. Once the king dreamt that the princess turned against him and killed him. And then he woke up. The dream

---

3   Reb Nachman, or Rebbe Nachman (1772-1810), great-grandson of Israel ben Eliezer, the Baal Shem Tov, founder of the Hassidic movement. Born in Ukraine, Reb Nachman is one of the movement's great masters. In his teachings, he combines secrets of the Cabbala with a deep understanding of the Torah.

*penetrated deep into his heart. So he summoned all
the dream interpreters. And they interpreted the dream
according to its simplest meaning: the dream would
come true in its simplest sense, and the princess would
kill him. So the king didn't know what to do with
her. Killing her would cause him suffering, but if he
banished her, someone else would take her, and that
too would disturb him greatly, for he had worked so
hard to get her, and now she would go to someone else
and the dream that she would kill him might come
true, for she would be with someone else. So the king
didn't know what to do. Meanwhile, his love for the
princess slowly waned because of the dream (that is,
he no longer loved her as before) and his love grew
smaller and smaller. And she also began to love him
less and less, until eventually she hated him. So she
ran away from him. The king ordered them to search
for her. And they came to him and told him she was
in the Water Castle, for there is a Water Castle with
ten walls, one inside the other, and all ten walls are
of water, and the castle floor, where you walk on it, is
also of water, and so is the garden with its trees, and
the fruit is all of water. And the princess, who had
run away, reached the Water Castle and was walking
around it. And they told the king that she was walking
around the Water Castle. So the king went with his
soldiers to capture her. As soon as the princess saw this,
she thought she would jump inside the castle, for she
would rather drown than be captured by the king and*

have to stay with him. And maybe she would save herself and could go into the Water Castle.

As soon as the king saw her running towards the water, he said: "Well, if that's the way it's going to be..." So he ordered them to shoot her, and if she died, so be it. So they shot her. And all ten kinds of poison struck her and she, the princess, threw herself into the Water Castle and entered it and went through all the gates of the water walls, for there are gates on the water walls, and she went through all the gates of all ten walls of the Water Castle, until eventually she entered the Water Castle and there she fell and lay lying without strength.

Who is this princess, and who is this old king?

The princess is our soul, or our "being" in the abstract sense. The old king is the Evil Impulse, or desire itself. Up until a certain point in our lives, we are completely enthralled with our desires. They guide our existence. Actually, they will always be the agenda of our existence but not with the passion or total surrender we experience in our childhood.

The stage of total confidence in our desires is eaten away by experience itself. As we exercise life, we realize we won't achieve the efficacy or wellbeing we want by always giving in to our desires. Desire has the sacred role of making us want and get, but it can be dangerous and destructive to the organism we manage, that is, to our being.

12

This discovery is shocking and confusing. All the queries (*fragues*) of our lives had been answered and our being had been formatted by the information we gathered while we were yielding to our desires. How are we to envisage a new stage of life without the guidance of this inner mother, of this instinct and will, which we identify as the primordial source of our survival?

Reb Nachman captures this drama brilliantly. Enraptured by his beloved, who he possesses, the king has a nightmare. The nightmare represents ambivalence, or the existence of two conflicting desires. The king prophesizes in this dream that the princess – his own soul -- would attempt to kill him in the future. This progressive betrayal manifests itself in a growing disillusionment about wanting mine to be mine and yours to be mine as well.

This guideline had governed our lives until this moment, and now we see it's not so adept at the task of preserving our organism. The adaptive intelligence of our brain—or perhaps we should say of our being—realizes our desire is a mother/lover who is dangerous and yet deeply loved. This creates an ambivalence that will be the new driving force behind questions about being and our way of having in the world.

In the story, desire realizes it is slowly being replaced by a new guideline. The perception that it will be killed is both false and true. It is false because desire is irreplaceable in interactions between our organism and the world. But it is true in the sense that a betrayal

Nilton Bonder

occurs, and desire will have to share its beloved with another guideline. Such sharing is incompatible with the nature of desire, and this is why ambivalences appear and force the princess to flee.

This is when the Evil Impulse reveals its full power. Until now, desire had merged with being—it was a mad passion. But being "flees," proving bigger than immediate desire and independent from it. There are desires that go beyond the immediate moment, strange desires that don't want to have what is wanted to be had. Immediate desire—the Evil Impulse—resists this betrayal and feels ambivalent towards his beloved. She used to be the absolute object of his love, and from this the king derived much good (many goods!). But now he's not concerned only about his beloved but about his unconditional possession of her. The king will not hesitate to hurt or harm the princess, for he has begun following his own agenda, an agenda no longer shared by the two of them but his alone—and the princess knows this. Perfect, virile, and idealized until this moment, her lover proves to be cruel and potentially abusive. And the princess—being—protects herself... protects her self from herself.

How ambivalent!

Here we see the ambivalence of the term "Evil Impulse," sacred and diabolical at the same time; the only way we can deal with it is by accepting this ambiguity. Any attempt to characterize it as only sacred or only demoniacal will close the door on the *shailas* (questions/ambivalences) of this new stage. And these *shailas* nourish survival and affirm our being. There is no avoiding them. If we see desire as only sacred, we become prisoners of a destructive way of life, or one that offers us less than life can offer us. After all, "what's mine is mine" means I am not willing to live less. I have no intention of tossing aside what's mine. But if, however, life offers me something I can't attain relying solely on the will of my immediate desire, then, sorry to say, the king will be betrayed. On the other hand, if desire is demonized, everything that it formatted and configured will become an enemy inside us, and we will not have a being to exercise. We will feel lost and will be turning our backs on the most sacred parameter of our being, which is desire. We will also be forfeiting "what is mine," and that is unconceivable.

The princess flees. This is the key feature of this stage.

The princess flees because she knows that an impulse which can no longer be an absolute lord or an exclusive lover becomes an impulse prone to evil. The terrified princess realizes she cannot trust her impulse alone. A guilty betrayer, her soul makes the only choice possible: it chooses itself. But what does it mean to choose oneself if this option is not merged with desire?

In his tale, Reb Nachman uses the image of a water castle into which the soul-princess throws herself. This frightening leap, which we must all take from time to time, is a leap of faith. For Reb Nachman, the water castle that saves the princess is the Torah, the Scriptures, the guidelines of our values. The waters represent the Torah, the world of values that seeks to safeguard our being by mediating between desire and its potential to turn into an Evil Impulse; better put perhaps, the waters represent life, or the Tree of Life.

Our whole experience of being is circumscribed within the realm of the Tree of Knowledge (which is also the Tree of Good and Evil). The entire construction of our being is based on the organic intelligence that creates markers of good and evil for the things of the world. Our senses are all built using these markers, which contrast things with things and define criteria. These criteria find material expression in our sight, our hearing, and our sense of smell or touch, but every so often we have to leap into another world, into a living void of waters that is no longer organic—that is, no longer built on structure or wisdom—but made of life.

Wisdom depends on a body, on an organism. Life does not. Life has another agenda and will transform this body to make it fit the agenda. In other words, being is not the final object, something we will explore in the last of the four realms: the spiritual.

This is the surprise (dream-nightmare) we discover: that we hold within us information or imperatives that will transform us, and the body from which our desire emanates will no longer be the same for the rest of our existence.

This is when the princess throws herself into the living unknown of the waters—the palace of waters. This palace is the Good Impulse. It is the new king, different from the old. The adulteress, ambivalent soul-princess will have two lovers, who she will have to reconcile: one will be her lover one moment and the other her spouse, and then they will switch roles, depending on the moment and occasion.

How can life present us with this adulteress, ambiguous situation?

Yet this appears to be its proposal, that is, unfaithfulness to both lovers and disobedience to immutable models of the kind "till death do them part." From time to time, we find that life is using us beyond any aspect of our being. And in this voluptuous current, our being has to find ways of being and establishing its identity inside a mutant body.

In the story, the soul-princess is saved in the palace of waters, but not before being pierced by ten arrows and ten poisons. Each one of the Ten Commandments of value will leave blemishes on our beings, and these wounds will last a lifetime...wounds that will be *shailas*, that is, ambivalences. But instead of abandoning us, lost, these ambivalences will in fact constitute us and configure us for a new stage of life. New acts of possession are now possible, as is a new form of desire, hybrid and no longer grounded solely in the body that says "what's mine is mine and what's yours is mine," but that glimpses the need for "yours to be yours."

YOURS IS YOURS

This new aspect of possession is wonderful. Understanding the concept that what's yours is yours introduces us to a new order in the universe. Desire still wants what's yours to be mine, but the Good Impulse shows us a new kind of need, a need unlike the experience of not wanting your friend's toy because he's stronger and you're afraid you'll get paid with a shove. This desire not to have is new because it takes the other person's desire into account, discarding the notion of possession as something confined solely to one individual.

Desire eventually discovers that the world is made up not only of things, but of things that desire too. And in order to gain possession of certain things that also desire, we have to join our desires to their desires. This is a new order of possession: for us to have, we must accept the fact that others also have.

This is not a benevolent or praiseworthy moral attitude but a practical adjustment to the world around us. Morality and culture are valuable tools in constructing the discourses and views that advance this new approach to possession. Yet they are not responsible for the concrete sustenance of this new paradigm that now becomes part of an individual's experience. No one obeys the law simply because disobeying it will redound in physical or psychological punishment. This only works to a very limited extent and under certain circumstances. Laws are obeyed because an individual believes they are important and favorable to him. This entails moral insight, that is, a new intelligence that while still organic transcends the individual.

As the word itself so nicely says, affection expresses things that affect me about you. A child does not love his parents by letting them sleep longer so they are rested. Any attempt to envision children as complying with such moral projections of our own does not accurately reflect how they experience life. This experience of affection, of emotional bonding, is focused on "mine is mine" but in a world where the component "yours" becomes increasingly useful in the act of possessing.

"What's yours is yours" is a concession we make so we can have the other. Since the other is an other who also wants to have, and since this is undeniably a requirement for taking possession, then let him have it. This in no way abolishes the constant impulse to make yours mine. But I resist this impulse, ambivalently, and I win "yours is yours" as a possession valuable to my being. Nor does this mean that everything the other wants is acceptable. Nor does this mean that we'll spend a good share or all of our lives trying to possess "things that desire" without accepting the plenitude of their desires. But we will have to find a way to reconcile the two, because these "things that desire" will try to win out, not forfeiting their "what's mine is mine."

"What's yours is yours" allows encounters to happen.

These encounters are vital because they are what give birth to partnerships and the collectivity; more importantly, they allow us to find companions for emotional projects—first and foremost, of course, the project of procreation. In order to mate, we must admit that what's yours is yours. Even in radical cultures, where men are given inordinate, abusive power and women are practically transformed into objects devoid of their own desires, courtship takes place and it is tacitly recognized that there is a space to be filled by a partner. The other can still be taken or possessed through rape, but any love that will allow a partnership to be built will have to recognize giving.

Just as it is necessary to learn to have as well as not to have in order to maximize possession, I have to accept the fact that what's yours is yours if I want to maximize what's mine is mine. This emotional intelligence kindles courtship, which represents the mating of desires manifested by two desiring entities. The inability to mate these desires bespeaks insufficient development; that is, it means you have trouble optimizing what's mine is mine. In order to achieve possession in this dimension, at some level you have to give. You have to make room, on top of your usual efforts to get room. This act of making room, or of recognizing needs that lie outside your own yet still matter to you, finds its most radical expression in the parent-child relationship.

But even here, we come up against the imperative of possession. It will always be hard for parents—and especially for mothers—to keep from possessing their children in a way that doesn't let them have what is theirs. Even in this kind of love, which is expressed by making room and by giving, we find the ambivalence of wanting to possess.

But loving parents know how to avoid such childish, physical possession, transforming it into an emotional possession that tolerates kinds of "having" that may clash with their own. The son who decides to become a musician instead of a doctor may challenge the possessive expectations of his mother or father, who dreamt about this triumph/possession. The greater our tolerance, the greater our ability to experience emotional ambivalence and the more loving our figure as parent, lover, friend, or compatriot is.

It is important for us to recognize that giving is always conditional in the emotional realm. The unconditional is not emotional because what is emotional belongs to the dimension of "what's mine is mine and yours is yours." We are only willing to accept that yours is yours if mine is mine. This is why love always involves some form of fidelity. It might be the weakest fidelity imaginable, but without it, there will be no bond and no partnership. Unconditional love is not part of the emotional realm but of another, as we will see later. This unconditional aspect cannot be achieved through emotions because, by definition, it entails an exchange. In the emotional realm, loving the other does not suffice; our love cannot go unrequited – we must get something in return. Even love that is willing to sacrifice—its own life at times— expects reciprocity; in other words, I expect that I will be able to keep some of the other as mine.

When you are betrayed, you feel hurt because you've been denied something that was yours. The emotional bond has been broken because the other was unable to fulfill the counterpart of "what's mine is mine." When, for example, our society returns to models of open relationships that strip love of any kind of possession, it is evident that this is not about expressing emotions but has to do with the intellectual realm instead. It is not surprising that couples who enter into such relationships are invariably intellectuals. These models bear resemblance to "mine is yours and yours is mine," as we will see later on.

If it is emotional, it must be reciprocal. Of course, there are less intense forms of exchange, and not all emotional modalities will involve building a family or sharing an apartment. These other modalities may adopt different conventions and maintain certain aspects of freedom. But whatever form they take, they will have to be corresponded. It is this right to reciprocity that characterizes emotional bonds. However much "mine" there is, the same amount of "yours" must be respected. Precise behavior patterns may vary, but all of them will have to respect this reciprocity. For example, some people do not form any bonds because they have trouble dealing with emotional ambivalence, preferring total physical possession of the other instead, for as long as possible. This turns the other into an object bereft of desire, someone requisitioned. And so we hear new slang like "friends with benefits." Expressions like these describe relationships with the lowest possible degree of emotional commitment, which turn sexuality or companionship into a physical commodity, one of absolute possession—mine is mine and yours is mine. Such choices radically hinder true possession, and the bonds tend to fade easily.

Others are happy just to flirt or entertain the false impression that they are always open to the opportunities presented by each moment. However, if there is no level of risk—which lies in ambivalence, exchange, and bonding—these people will never exercise possession. Unable to detach themselves from the physical realm, such people fall prey to fetishes, which are a false feeling of possession. A fetish plays the role of keeping someone else from possessing; but by denying that person the right to be the other, it will not be possible to possess him in the emotional realm.

The new values of our emotional world will be defined by reciprocity. This "you" will be the other, who is no longer "it" but now has the right to what is "yours is yours." Dialogue and relationships are fostered through this partnership. All types of families and societies are built out of this mature attitude towards the issue of possession.

This reciprocity demands a faithfulness that is in itself the great betrayal of the Evil Impulse. The old king knows how dangerous it is to draw up contracts and create expectations that are repressive for him and that condemn his constant desire to possess without compromise. Our love for others will always conflict with our love of ourselves. To love means never abandoning this ambivalence. People who become emotionally involved and hand their desire (their Evil Impulse) over to the other are throwing out their chance for emotional possession and regressing to a childish, physical possession, which tries to do away with ambivalence and neutralize it through self-sacrifice. This modality of camouflaged possession is nothing more than an effort to assign childish possession of our self to the other; it represents an act of capitulation and renunciation that can lead to depression and illness. Unless we possess ourselves, and unless we possess in general, we cannot be, and depending upon the degree of this interdiction, it even can endanger our life.

Loving means standing on the threshold of betraying oneself or the other. It is by correcting and adjusting these tiny, never-ending acts of betrayal that we can "be" emotionally. Being bears a direct relation to how much we have of ourselves and of the other, ambivalently intertwined in a bond between two organisms that use each other mutually and nourish each other mutually. There is no way to "be" without interaction. The emotional realm represents the marriage of the soul to the old king and the young king, to the Evil Impulse and the Good Impulse. Within this tense, ambiguous bigamy, we experience the blessings of what is "mine is mine and yours is yours."

It is vital for us to understand that the emotional world is a world of values still explicitly based on receiving. It is not a world of giving, though we usually hear this preached. Herein lies the great beauty and vitality of the emotional world. Even with its compromises, it is still a world of possession whose prime characteristic is taking. Taking, but not without being wounded by ten arrows.

Chapter III

Intellectual Realm

To Have or Not to Have? — That is the
kashia (doubt)!

WHAT'S MINE IS YOURS — WHAT'S
YOURS IS MINE

With the passage of time, the greatest potential for
being shifts from the physical to the emotional realm,
and then from the emotional to the intellectual. The
brain and mental faculties come to form a human being's
most robust organic features. In the course of our life
experiences, our ability to discern patterns in the world
and the reality around us unleashes our intellectual
potential, which moves onto center stage during this
new phase. Of course, our mental side is present during

all other phases too, as are our physical, emotional, and spiritual sides, but now, because our intellect has reached maturity, it dictates the tendencies of the moment and gives our brains tremendous influence.

I am not talking about rationality; on the contrary, these patterns almost always challenge and run counter to rationality. A philosopher is not rational; his interest and studies lie in rationality's discontinuities and in the rough edges between mental structures, concepts, and reality. Where thought and the world do not dovetail, there lies "being." There lie the distortions born during the experience of being.

This is a rather intriguing aspect of existence. As long as there are illusions—that is, discrepancies between vision and reality, between version and fact— there we will find life; there we will find the experience of being. Illusions are the greatest proof of existence, the greatest proof that in this particular place in the universe we will encounter the phenomenon of desire, impelled by organic demands that place greater weight on their internal wills and wishes for possession than on the surrounding reality. Life is the locus where illusion is possible. And although illusion is a distortion—just as the presence of a body deforms or distorts time-space—the experience of being finds expression within it. Our desires to have, which generate illusions, are the flip side of the same coin that allows us to experience being.

All types of therapy play this role: they help the patient manage his diverse experiences by helping him perceive the illusions and deformations around him. What was "mine" and did not become "mine" (those famous injustices) can only be determined in this place where there is life. Possession—or, more accurately, our desire for possession—is the only consistent proof of life. Where this desire does not exist, no organism exists, nor does life exist. Life is defined by possession, and no other category is so peculiar and unique to life.

The primary place for illusions is the mental realm, where human illusions are sustained. And this is the mental realm's biggest role in our survival: to produce a political and strategic platform for life. It is no accident that these mental designs will endeavor to develop a sense of justice. I can express my demands on life and legitimize my right to possession within the framework of justice. So the mental realm always tries to respond not only to the queries generated by our demands for possession but also to the emotional ambivalences associated with possession.

Many of our acts of possession take place in this mental dimension. A vast amount of moral literature deals with the illusion of possession. It tells us there is no possession and everything belongs to God; we are only tenants, temporary users, without any right to possess anything in this universe. As much as this morality may represent an effort to correct the illusions we produce while trying to better adjust "being" to the world, it cannot be considered absolute. Do away with the illusions caused by existence and "being" is gone. Being is the cause of these illusions. It is essential to reshape these illusions so they reward us with as much wellbeing as possible, without rendering existence unviable within a real, non-illusory environment. But to wipe out these illusions, to wholly explain them away, would annihilate being. The universal convention for defining the moment of death is the cessation of mental activity, or "brain death." I would go so far as to say that what defines death is our incapacity to create illusions—in other words, to create the distortions generated by our desire for our self, by our desire to have.

While the physical world expresses "mine is mine and yours is mine," and the emotional world tries to reconcile "mine is mine and yours is yours," the mental, intellectual world curiously ventures into the abstract possibility that "mine is yours and yours is mine." The so-called economic market, with its financial investments, jumbles possessions up in a complicated, illusory way; this is part of the mental realm. When we come to understand this knotted tangle of possession, we discover an important component of the experience of being vis-à-vis having.

So far in our examination, possession has been restricted to the present time. In the physical and emotional realms, the desire for possession is always present. Whether material or emotional, desire is an expression of the moment; there is no other time.

29

Physical and emotional desires are concrete, because they are manifested and can only be satisfied in the here and now. In none of these desires can we conceive the possibility that "what is mine may be yours." This notion is conceptual, abstract, and extrapolates the here and now. At this moment, the only thing that exists is the concrete "mine is mine," "yours is mine," or, at most, "yours is yours." It's impossible to find any meaning in "mine is yours" within the here and now but only within our projection into the future.

The mental realm actually invents the future, which is simply a conceptual notion, a chessboard where we engage in exploration and analyses, trying to anticipate coming events. Here in this virtual place we process the choice that will enable us to imagine that "what's mine is yours."

WHAT'S MINE IS YOURS — WHAT'S YOURS IS MINE

Present time cannot relinquish the concept of "what's mine is mine." Within the emotional realm, the most the present can encompass is the idea that "what is yours is yours." In the physical realm, everything will always have to be "mine," whether it's mine or yours. Of course, we cannot wield our power of possession over everything. We run up against the other person's desire, and the other will protect what is his and not let us possess it. But even if we don't have it, we still hold out hope that "what's yours will be mine." We never lose this hope, even if intervening forces impose something quite contrary to our desire. The physical realm wants for itself, always.

In the emotional realm, when we perceive that "yours is yours," we do so in the hopes of gaining possession of the other. This possession is no longer an interaction with something static but with another human being, and thus it presupposes a relationship. We will not be loved if we do not give in to the other's demands. This reward, which lets the other have as we have, is not conceptual and contains no element of judgment as far as rights or merit. It is a simple symbiosis in which we find use for the other, accepting that he will bring his own desires with him. Love is our perception that we are dependent on the other, and this dependence forces us to accept the fact that this other also wants "what is his to be his." This negotiation is always ambivalent because it asks us to respect interests beyond our own identity or person, but these ambivalent interests are what allow for possession within the realm of emotion.

A new possibility arises in the mental realm: that "mine is yours." However, this first element of donation can only come as an offer if coupled with the expectation that "yours is mine." There can be no absolute rendering or surrendering in the realm of a demand in the here and now; giving and solidarity can only take place outside the anticipation for exchange. It is impossible for us to imagine giving when we are under the influence of a demand in the here and now; giving becomes possible through exchange and solidarity. I'll give to you if you give to me. I'll make you a loan if you make me a loan. This equity makes it possible to forego in order to have. It is precisely within the mental realm that the market of exchange becomes feasible. Trades are not ambivalent because they are symmetrical. Trades create "doubts," as we will see later. There is no ambivalence in a trade because the yours isn't yours; it's the mine that ended up being yours, since yours ended up being mine. The mental realm doesn't have to recognize the other because it doesn't need to gain possession of it; instead, it interacts with the other in order to expand possession.

The mental realm is parallel to the physical realm at a subtler level, just as the spiritual realm is parallel to the emotional, likewise at a subtler level. The mental realm devises ways to gain further possession, through investment beyond immediate possession. We can conceive of the future thanks to our mental faculty of perceiving causes and consequences. Our ability to anticipate consequences arms us with the ability to build models. Created through the perception of patterns, these models enable me to see that I will gain greater possession, or that more will be mine, if I make mine yours for a moment, so that later I can make yours mine. This is the principle behind interest on money and behind all types of dividends.

The purpose of this world is to conceive of a greater, broader possession, arising within the mental realm. We are not talking about possessing something or someone but of possessing potential possessions, that is, the kind of possession needed to meet demands that don't exist yet. The mental realm somehow glimpses the possibility of gaining possession of possession itself.

Behind the idea that "what's mine is yours and yours is mine" lies the desire for security. This is the design that our organic intelligence perceives in the possibility of the future. Until the notion of future had been constructed, possession was tied solely to our desire of the moment and to the real possession of something. From now on, however, it can also rely on virtual possession. This virtual possession is not what I want now—the Evil

Impulse—but what I may come to want later. Security is the goal of possession. The novelty of this stage is that possession no longer must be characterized by a need in the here and now but by any possession that might occur in the future. This is quite likely the organic condition that allows for the conception of money. Money represents the mental possession of something I don't need yet; more precisely, it represents the possibility of making possession transcend merely physical needs.

This is why the mental realm is a refined version of the physical realm; it is a physical realm with an aggregate value. If the physical realm represents everything I have to manage about myself, the mental realm invents an even greater physical realm that must be managed. We're talking about everything the physical realm could need in the here and now, plus everything it might come to need in the future. And this new desire with an aggregate value no longer corresponds to what I want now, but to what I may come to want. This new relation to possession is no longer ambivalent because it brings the "question" back into the realm of the self. Now the other is no longer a partner whose desire should be respected, but an instrument through which I can maximize my possession.

The other and the market we engage in together expand the possibilities of possession. For one thing, I can take from you for myself (yours is mine) via solidarity, which reciprocally means you can take from me (mine is yours). Moreover, I can also resort to exploitation and, on non-equal terms, make yours more mine than I allow mine to be yours.

This is the design perceived by the organic mental realm: "mine is yours and yours is mine" matters to me because it allows me to enjoy the benefits of security and exploitation. Both forms add aggregate value to possession. Yes, it does indeed leave me vulnerable to exploitation myself; in other words, it may be that more "mine will be yours" than "yours will be mine." It doesn't matter. The risk, or the possibility of gain or of adding value to my possession, is attractive enough that I'll chance it—after all, what is organic is programmed to seek even in the face of risk, which is the best way of managing oneself.

Note that this attitude is not destructive in and of itself; it is organic. Wanting to exploit someone else simply means we have discovered that the other is not merely an object to be possessed but can be a constant producer of other acts of possession for ourselves. And in a way, societies are built with these two aims: solidarity or exploitation. Of course, our justification for joining these societies is that they offer us a chance to benefit from solidarity. Mine can be yours, if one day yours can be mine. For example, when the elderly retire, some rely on solidarity; others, on exploitation. The former are those who worked when they were younger to support the elders of their day. After making mine yours, they reap the benefit of yours being mine. True, inequalities can occur, and other people may end up working harder or longer, so that they make more "yours is mine" than "mine is yours." This societal proposal begins with a desire for solidarity and exploitation. Only when we end up relinquishing more of "mine" than someone else cedes in the form of "yours" do we complain and question the validity, or the design, of this mental scheme.

This intellectual game may be taken as a regression to physical concepts, for it is as if "mine is yours and yours is mine" were built on a hidden desire for "mine to be mine and yours to be mine." This physical desire will never be superseded; it will always be the background of our existence. It was present in the emotional dimension and in the mental as well. This desire is not immoral but simply organic. It is always in the name of the organic that we are good or loving. Whenever we assign a value to an act or behavior, it is always to advance the cause of the individual and his imperative to manage himself.

It is not because of our motivations that this model generates "questions." The main problem is that possession projected into the future may not represent a true desire. Although I may save money for my own security or to satisfy some potential future desire, my plans may not always come to fruition. And if my needs do not prove real, there will be no organic reason for my possession and I will have taken possession of something that will never become a good. And taking possession of something that we will not "have" seriously jeopardizes the structure of what is "mine." Any effort or energy wasted in getting something I will not have is an attack on being, and it rents asunder the intrinsic relation between having and being. "Doubts" appear.

DOUBTS — *KASHIA*

Doubt differs greatly from a query (*frague*) or ambivalence (*shaila*). Life itself raises the question. Our decisions to advance or retreat, to expand or contract, to attack or flee, are reactions to the 'problem statements' of life itself. Survival requires us to make these decisions, but it isn't up to us to do anything more than respond and react to the situations that come our way. Even ambivalences are no more than a sub-group of questions wherein contradictions and complexities arise; but ambivalences also prompt a search for answers within the bounds of what life throws our way. Doubt, however, is a product not only of our problem-solving efforts but also of our efforts to alter life's problem statements. The mental realm and its virtual trait not only embraces the real possibilities that appear before it—the "questions" that life posits—but also creates models and proposes new problems. "And what if it were like this or like that?" a human being wonders. But if things aren't like that, why concern ourselves or delve into conditions that don't exist? The answer is that we do this because of the possibility of possessing.

The Book of Genesis and its narrative about Adam and Eve eating from the Tree of Knowledge is rife with tension. But this tension doesn't stem from the fact that Adam and Eve resorted to the Tree's fruit in an effort to deal with life's questions and ambivalence. It stems instead from the fact that human beings were less concerned about seeking wise answers to their questions than about meddling with the Tree of Life and questioning the wisdom of Creation itself. Casting aside their status as mere creatures, they wanted to critique Creation itself. They authorized themselves to act as consultants – even more, as people who could judge Creation and propose a better one. In *A Reforma da Natureza* (Reforming Nature), Brazilian writer Monteiro Lobato captures the ability of the human imagination to propose new problem statements and to wish for problems flexible enough to fit desired solutions. Instead of grappling with "imperfections", it seems easier to change demands and proposals and expand the boundaries of perfection to suit our interests.

This is why people today no longer ask how to cure diseases but whether sometime it will be possible to do away with them. Genetic engineering no longer thinks just about the limits of a cure but about the end of the problem statement that proposes aging and death. While queries and ambivalences ask "How?" "When?" "Where?" "Which?" or "Can I?", doubts spring from the audacity of asking: "Why?" Who decided these would be the problem statements I'd have to cope with?

When the human spirit decided to tackle structures and speculate about itself and its condition as relative rather than absolute, it turned itself and the world into an open project, making individuality and reality a mystery. But there is no mystery in the world. Mystery is the intercession between human desire and reality, between the hope for justice and fate.

Such is the ordeal of the human being who takes of the forbidden fruit: he cannot honor himself without his illusions and his mystery. And so the human being has surrounded himself with doubts about himself and the world. The most popular doubt has to do with God— whether God exists or not. But notice how misplaced this "doubt" is; it hides our true angst, which is "do I exist or not?"

Any proof of the existence of God will rely on the logic inherent to our concept of justice and order, which generally sides with me and my possessions. God exists so long as my desires take precedence over reality. In other words, do I deserve not only answers to my questions about life but also the right to change problem statements to better fit my demands? The mental realm produces doubts—*kashias*—and they plague our "to be or not to be." And are we? And is the world? And did the Creator create? Each and every parameter can be made relative when doubt causes a feeling of angst to infect our very sense of self. When we challenge limits and boundaries, demarcated territory ceases to exist and indefinition gains more power.

What lie behind this whole world of experiences is the mental realm and its ability to abstract and to produce models. The same mental faculty that animates new areas of human skill also intensifies uncertainty and produces doubts. This in turn generates new queries, which are structural in nature. The question deals no longer with finding food but how much to eat; or no longer how to survive our fate but questioning this fate; or no longer how to account for myself but questioning who I am and why am I like this.

This is particularly apparent to us with possession: What might be mine even though I don't need it right now? In earlier stages, possession represented my momentary control over something necessary to my survival. Now it no longer has limits; it has become a never-ending conquest that will satisfy my doubts and lend me my individuality. Possession isn't tied to my set of needs here and now anymore but to the whole new set of demands that the future might generate.

The mental world is capable of valuing not only the present but also of attempting the unbelievable challenge of valuing the future. But how can we value demands that don't even exist yet? How can we assign prices to the future when the future is not real but a virtual construction that replaces immediate experience with models? This only became possible with the advent of money. Money enables us to have, detached from the possession of something real. The human being devised a powerful tool for expanding his demands for possession, no longer just physical and emotional but mental as well.

Money makes what's mine yours and what's yours mine, because money has no object of possession save the virtual of everything it may come to buy and be transformed into. When I have a ten-dollar bill in my hands, I have mine and yours, and you, with your ten-dollar bill, have yours and mine. We both have possession and neither of us has possession. Consequently, queries and ambivalences become doubts. The former were about possession in and of itself; now our questions are about the subject of possession. Who is this person who can have what he doesn't need? What lends legitimacy and reason to this possession if the definition of the subject changes? What is its existential value, and how can reality embrace solutions for which there are as yet no problems? Do problem statements built out of solutions have any value? Or is there any value in supply for which there is as yet no demand? These are our doubts.

MONEY —
THE POTENTIAL TO HAVE WITHOUT HAVING

Until the advent of money, the notion of possession encompassed the sum total of an object's uses and utilities. Possession meant no one could use this object without my permission. But money has turned the desired object into an economic object. So the relation between money and real things cannot be accurately determined. It is only when money wants to meet a real demand in the here and now that its value is put to the test. Hence, money strips possession of substance and turns it into a function—the possession of possession. Through money, possession can become static rather than dynamic in nature, constantly determined by life's exchange between potential supply and demand. Money creates a rift in the dependent relationship between having and being, since having is no longer tied to the being of another object nor to the being of someone who as yet has no demand for the supply represented by this money.

Money elevates the idea of the Evil Impulse to a higher level of complexity. As stated earlier, the Evil Impulse represents a demand detached from a value. Satisfying an immediate demand without being aware of potential losses as well as potential gains—without knowing the costs involved, i.e., its value—represents the Evil Impulse. The ability to postpone immediate demands in favor of more valuable demands represents the Good Impulse and the ability to exercise our free will to have or not have while taking all values into account—not just material and physical ones but emotional, ethical, and spiritual ones as well.

Money, however, can disguise itself as a value, pretending we are relinquishing the possibility of immediate gratification for something of greater worth in the future. In reality, it makes us believe that to have money is to have possessions. In a way, money evades or sidesteps the question of having OR not having, because money is a form of having AND not having. Money embodies the doubts that only the mental realm can produce. It is a doubt about being itself, whose relation to having seems to disappear. Yet it would be very naïve to place any responsibility on money, which is simply a means—a construct of the human being's mental dimension. A rope, a hammer, or a gun is not responsible for what it does. Behind these lies a Being who is not a victim of money but its inventor. And so all money and the whole increasingly complex financial market express this immense doubt bred within the mental world. If I make mine yours and you make yours mine, can I increase my possessions? But if mine is yours and yours is mine, if our possessions are conflated so that I can have more possession, who am I?

This is the same question we ask when our mental realm has us thinking about ourselves in relation to the future. In the physical and emotional realms, our image and our experience of being are always in the present. The mental world proposes constructs about the future and establishes complex relations about who I am. And what if I do this or that? And what if the result is this or that? And what if I have or if I don't have? And so on. Yet as contradictory as it may seem, this is precisely how the mental realm relates being to having. In the mental world, being is not an experience of the here and now, but a complex relationship between present and future. From this perspective, money translates into the mental manifestation of possession. We are not talking about a possession that has any value in the present moment; we're talking about a value that lends the future the same legitimacy of the here and now when it comes to evaluating costs and benefits. In this sense, security and liquidity are mental possessions that meet mental demands of both the present and the future.

Insurance and pension funds are included among a human being's possessions in the modern world, where the mental realm finds social and economic expression. They are part of what we feel we possess, and as such— as mental possessions—they are part of our balance sheets and inventories. Certainties and guarantees are forms of possession in the mental world because they value not only the present but also its speculations about the future. We therefore recognize as "goods" not just

45

what is useful in the present but also what may come to be useful in the future in order to satisfy demands that currently exist only in conceptual terms.

Within the mental realm, what then is our *kashia*—our doubt—about having? Or to put it another way, what is the doubt that having or not having poses for the experience of being within this dimension?

A brief story by Reb Nachman of Breslov can help us gain a deeper understanding of the elaborate relationship between being and having—or between what we want to have and not to have in the mental world—and the implications for being.

There once was a King who loved to dress in the clothing of commoners and pass himself off as one of his subjects. He did this to get to know the ordinary people of his kingdom.

One day the King found himself in a poorer area of the city, and in the distance he heard a melody. He thought: "A song in such a poor place—surely it is a lament."

However, as he grew nearer the source of the melody, he realized it was a happy song! And it was coming from the poorest shack on the street.

He knocked on the door and asked, "Is a stranger welcome here?"

A voice from inside said: "A stranger is a gift from God!"

In the dim light the King saw a man sitting there sewing a shoe. He asked: "What do you do?"

"I'm a shoemaker," the man replied.

"Do you have a shop where you make shoes?" the King asked.

"No, I can't afford a shop. I take my toolbox and go out on the sidewalk. When someone needs me, I fix their shoes," the man said.

"And do you make enough to support yourself?" the King inquired.

The man humbly replied, "I only earn enough to support myself day by day."

"Only enough for a day? Don't you worry that one day you won't have enough and you'll go hungry?" the King asked.

"Blessed be the Creator, day by day," came the reply.

The next day, the King decided to put this man's philosophy of life to the test. He proclaimed that all shoemakers on the street would need a license that cost 50 gold pieces.

That night, he went back to the man's house and from afar heard the shoemaker humming an even happier tune. The King knocked at his door and commented, "My friend, I heard about the edict proclaimed by the mean King. I was worried about you. How did you manage to eat today?"

"I was upset when I learned I'd no longer be able to support myself like before, but I knew: 'I have the

right to support myself, and I will find a way to do
it.' While I was thinking about this, a group of people
went by. When I asked where they were headed, they
said they were going into the forest to gather branches
and wood.

"Every day they go out and collect firewood. When
I asked if I could go with them, they said, 'There's a
huge forest. Come along with us.'

"I gathered wood, and at the end of the day, I
managed to sell it and made enough to support myself
that day."

Surprised, the King exclaimed, "Just for one day?
And what about tomorrow? And next week?"

"Blessed is the Eternal One, day by day."

The next day the King went back to his throne and
issued another proclamation. Anyone seen gathering
firewood would be forced to serve in the Royal Guards.
And he added an amendment stating that members of
the guard would not be paid for 40 days.

That night the King went back to the poor
neighborhood and to his surprise heard an even
happier song. The King knocked on the door and asked,
"Shoemaker, how did your day go?"

"They made me stay on duty all day with the Royal
Guard. Then they gave me a sword and a sheath for
it. But then they told me I wouldn't be paid for 40
days!"

"I bet you thought you should have saved some
money, my friend," the King said smugly.

"Let me tell you what I did: I realized the blade of the sword must be worth something. So I took it off and attached a wooden stick to the handle. I thought to myself, inside the sheath, no one will be able to tell if it's metal or wood. I took it to the blacksmith and he bought the metal. I got enough money to survive another day."

The King was upset: *"And what will you do tomorrow if the swords are inspected?"*

The man replied: *"Blessed the Creator, day by day."*

The next day the King chose the shoemaker from among all the soldiers in the Royal Guard. The shoemaker didn't recognize the King, who said to him, *"Guard, this man here committed a violent crime. I want you to take him to the main square and cut his head off right now."*

The shoemaker tried to argue, *"Forgive me, Sir, but I am a peaceful man, I couldn't take someone else's life!"*

"If you don't do what I say, you'll both be killed."

Shaking, the poor shoemaker was taken to the middle of the square, surrounded by the crowd that had gathered to watch the execution. The shoemaker put the prisoner's head on a tree trunk and, with his hand on his sword, started to pull it out. Then he turned to the crowd and said:

"With God as my Witness, I am not a killer. If this man is guilty of the charges against him may my sword

49

*be as always; but if he is innocent, may my sword be
made into wood!"*

*He drew his sword and the people couldn't believe
it—the sword had been turned into wood. The people
bowed down in recognition of the great miracle they
had witnessed.*

*The King, who had watched it all, went up to the
shoemaker and took his hands. He said, "I am the King
and I am also the man who has visited you every night.
I want you to come live with me in the palace and be
one of my advisors. Please, teach me how to live like
this: one day at a time."*

This story contrasts the concept of "one day at a
time" with the meaning of money. Representing the
Evil Impulse within the mental realm, the King is
disguised as a beggar. In the physical and emotional
worlds, the Evil Impulse always encourages immediate
gratification. Yet here the King seems to be proposing
the opposite. He asks: "Don't you want to have more
than just your livelihood? How come you don't want
more?" He is apparently proposing that the shoemaker
not be so focused on his immediate needs. If you don't
need it now, you might need it later. Better the greed
that guarantees our future than only satisfying the
demands of the here and now. Accumulation is the Good
Impulse, the ability to forfeit now in order to enjoy later.
But in point of fact, this is the Evil Impulse deceiving
us within the mental dimension. Accumulation is not

necessarily about "not having" so that we may increase possession. It can be a false not having that appears to postpone gratification but really confuses a person; instead of fostering possession, it makes possession unviable. Furthermore, in addition to representing the Evil Impulse, the King represents identity in search of itself. In his desire to "learn" through the shoemaker, the King shows us how being suffers as it grapples with its incredible doubt.

The epicenter of a doubt lies in tomorrow's potential demands, since being does not exist in the future, except as a mental kind of "being." A king transformed into a penniless subject (a non-being) or into a King (a being in all its grandeur) represents the quest for identity. He envies the shoemaker, who in his physical and emotional dimensions is more real than the King. The King's "unreality" is his supreme "doubt." "Am I or am I not?" the King asks himself, because he has serious doubts about whether he has or does not have.

The King's doubt is compelling. By failing to make decisions about wanting to have or not have something, the King gradually distances himself from his sense of self and comes face to face with his insecurity and lack of identity. By not honoring his mental dimension, the King is left with the constant impression that he is a fool and that he is not making full use of all the possession meant for him in this world. Not utilizing it betrays his deepest organic sense and destabilizes his experience of being. At the same time, the mental realm constantly falls for notions like "money" that make us feel that we're not really, at each and every moment, choosing what we want or do not want to have. As we have seen, money can be a false possession. When we want to satisfy some demand in the present, we might want to change money into a real possession but discover it doesn't have enough value. We experience this sense of insolvency primarily in the present time, since this is the only thing money can't buy. Our efforts and the time we waste in worthless accumulation that cannot be translated into real demands are a tragedy. This is why the shoemaker bothers the King so much: while on the one hand the shoemaker has no way of guaranteeing his tomorrow, on the other, he neither consumes nor wastes today in search of any such guarantee.

The King believes that time is money, and the shoemaker, that money is time.

Money can bring freedom and time, but it cannot recover the specific present moment that was replaced by the search to satisfy the demands of the future. And herein lies our greatest doubt: If the mental realm achieves the feat of producing the experience of being in the future, how can we know if the Good Impulse—the desire to produce 'goods'—is not the Evil Impulse in disguise?

When we discover that under these circumstances the Evil Impulse—living now and not postponing—may be our best option for investing in greater possession, confusion and doubt are sown. It is not only our urge for immediate satisfaction that causes us to get ahead of ourselves and miss out on chances to invest in bigger possessions; sometimes it may also be the very act of postponing experiences of possession and of being in a given moment. These experiences cannot be reproduced and will be discarded as present time is transformed.

So what weights and measures do we use to physically and emotionally honor the here and now, at the same time that we mentally honor our expectations and strategies for increasing our possessions?

When divested of its moral guise, the fable of the Ant and the Grasshopper paints a sharp picture of doubt about possession in the mental world. To be an ant or to be a grasshopper? — That is the question. To be a King or to be a shoemaker? — That is the question. By question, obviously, we mean doubt.

In my passage through the world, I have met Kings in search of shoemakers' secrets, as well as shoemakers who are unhappy because they can't be Kings. One searches for simplicity and the other, runs away from the fate of being a simpleton. The story doesn't tell us what happened later. If the shoemaker accepted the King's proposal he probably ended up becoming like the King. That's the trouble with doubt—there's doubt about it. Morality uses doubts sometimes to tell us we should be shoemakers, and sometimes to tell us we should be Kings. The size of a human being cannot be a definitive achievement or source of enlightenment. If it could, it would represent the end of the experience of being. No one who avails himself of the mental world, for good or for bad, will be able to cope with this doubt; after all, it is in the mental world that we experience being.

In the mental world, being or not being is more than having or not having. It perhaps has more to do with what my size is and what it isn't. Since the mental realm is responsible for conceptual perception, it is there that we need to know our size and limitations, so we can value things and be. The future endows the mental dimension not only with the experience of being but also with the experience of what can be, because the King's potential pathology is wanting to be everything (more than he is or can have), while the shoemaker's is not being all that he is (or everything he can have).

There is no more evocative representation of this doubt than the rabbinical advice that we should carry two little notes around in our pockets: in one pocket, a sentence reading *"you are dust and to dust shall return"* and in the other *"the world was created for you"*. When we put our hand into one of the pockets, it reveals the here and now. Being (or not being) is not found in either pocket. Mentally, being lies in having both pockets and in having doubt. It is by experiencing this doubt that we can grasp our own existence. Those who are bigger than they are and those who are smaller than they are suffer identity crisis, that is, crisis of being. These are crises of possession: about how much of theirs they didn't take possession of and about how much they lost when they took possession while forfeiting something even more valuable. Perhaps what had greatest value was their time itself. If the "mine that is yours" was not an option but a renunciation because I didn't know my size, then I am not. If the "yours that is mine" is mine in proportions not befitting my size, then once again I have not achieved my appropriate potential.

In the physical world, this idea would be absurd. In moral terms, the physical world knows no waste, because the world of the here and now is circumscribed to the demands of the present. There is no way we can lose when endeavoring to satisfy the demands of the present; at worst, they won't be met—in other words, the here and now presents nothing but queries, and never will these take the form of doubts. When it comes to questions in the physical world, the King and the shoemaker are one single figure. In the mental world, they long for each other.

The King cannot be the mental model, wanting "mine to be mine and yours to be mine" both in the present and future as well. This is because future demands are infinite in size and their magnitude is inappropriate to a human being; in other words, the King's big problem is that when he mentally tries to be King, he is incompatible with being himself.

The shoemaker is not only optimistic, in contrast with the bored, depressed King; he is also creative and knows how to improvise. The shoemaker is a figure who is alive; his constant presence evinces a form of being envied by the King. Caught up in demands of the future, the King experiences less sparkle in the present—sparkle that the shoemaker shows off in his song and in his unshakable happiness.

It's hard for us human beings to recognize that our being is tied to our having. Moral tenets confuse us, because they try to make this relation seem ethical in nature when it is actually organic. Nothing illustrates this better than gluttony. Just as unpleasant as hunger pangs are the pains of a stuffed belly. One dreams about the other, while they really aspire to reach a balance that translates into wellbeing, a challenging balance that links possession to what we are. The closer we are to what befits us organically, the happier we are, and the more creative and more present. Like everything else, the mental dimension is an instrument of our wellbeing and also one of its greatest obstacles.

This is a longstanding human doubt that we constantly revisit: should we limit ourselves to our allotted portion or should we stuff ourselves at the banquet?

What measure of appropriation and "non-appropriation" will optimize possession?

Chapter IV

Spiritual Realm

To Have or Not to Have? — That is the
teiku (paradox)!

WHAT'S MINE IS YOURS — WHAT'S YOURS IS YOURS

By definition, the spiritual realm is the farthest removed from the physical realm. Yet this doesn't mean one is the antithesis of the other. Intertwined without any implicit hierarchy, the four worlds account for the organic structure in all its forms. The spiritual realm is the dimension of being that seems most independent from the physical component of our experience. It is the boundary of our being, best expressed through the nonexistence of demands for possession.

57

Since our bodies require possessions in order to exist, the more remote our experience of this body, the less it will be translated into possessions. Better put, the more our experience will find expression precisely through the absence of possessions.

Aging is a gradual organic abandonment of physical regeneration, which in and of itself constitutes the ultimate renunciation of possession—our possession of our self. During later periods of our lives, our living experience is the opposite of what it was during earlier years. We believe things are less important, because our body no longer has the vitality needed to enjoy the blessings of this world. However, aging is a structural aspect that comes from another model of renewal, which discards one generation and moves on to the next. Since the desire to possess is determined organically, as we age it should be replaced by an equally strong desire to transmit things and hand them down. Just as having defines being throughout much of our lives, not having is the organic response to a mature, well-balanced aging process.

If our old age is filled with desires for possession, it means we are engaged in a useless attempt to stave off death and resist our organism's new demands. Old age brings an amazing turnaround that only more sensitive people will perceive: what was spiritual before becomes physical now and vice versa. The physical realm loses touch with what had been its characteristic demands, and if we listen hard enough to our body, we will see that it asks for less because it processes less and because it develops mechanisms that don't involve expansion and growth but rather contraction and the loss of density. Our bodies move away from the physical realm, revealing the spiritual realm that had always been contained within them. Before, the spiritual realm went to the boundaries of the physical world to make subtler aspects of existence manifest; but now the most powerful tool for translating its "questions" is found within our bodies, which are renouncing themselves. These are not really questions but "paradoxes."

When the physical dimension renounces itself—in other words, acquires a non-material, non-corporeal manifestation—and when spirituality finds its natural place in our body, then we are up against a paradox. At this pole of existence, decisions involving identity, or being, find their gravitational center in the realm of not having. While the experience of being was formerly defined by what we wanted to have and what we wanted to not have, now the emphasis will be on not having. For in the past, the tough decisions had to do with giving up and learning what not to have; now they are about what we must have.

It is as if we transferred the sense of sacrifice that comes from forfeiting our desire for immediate satisfaction away from our decision to not have to the decision to have during this phase of life—when the great sacrifice becomes having. We often times hear someone urging an old person to eat more, make an effort to get out and be with other people, and, especially, not forget his wishes or forego his whims. It's as if the effort required in old age is not giving up but, to the contrary, taking and possessing.

In old age, possessing demands as much restraint as forfeiting did in our youth. When an old person takes up space or a project, this is an act of courage, just as it is an act of courage for a young person to cede to someone else or offer something up. As said in *Ethics of the Fathers*: "Strong is he who controls his passion." For a young man, having is his passion; for an old man, the passion is not having. And the elderly who are strong want to have with the same spirituality required by young folks who don't want to have.

This oblique view of having not only redefines our entire experience of being; it also helps us better understand life's ongoing relationship with possession. Possession reflects a dynamic, changing inner balance, which the organism perceives as its very existence. To exist means to measure and to manage having. We perceive this momentary, ongoing act as the experience of being. If you have less than befits you or more than befits you at a given moment, you will experience a feeling of absence. If you are in balance with what you possess in your here and now, you will experience a feeling of presence. As we have seen, and perhaps can better appreciate now, "to have or not to have is the question." From this perspective, in fact, we can appreciate that, more than a question, it is a paradox.

PARADOX — *TEIKU*

Paradoxes are apparent during old age but are present throughout our existence. Eastern tradition addresses paradox in its teachings on reality and illusion. The more we hold in our hands, the less we have. When we see having as the antithesis of being and the biggest object of our illusions, we are not admitting that having is a constant query, ambivalence, doubt, or even paradox. But the greatest life lesson lies precisely in licit or illicit appropriation. In its deepest sense, this word itself means that we should only appropriate what is appropriate" to us.

There are no limits to having except not having. This is an ecological principle. The best-adapted species have and don't have in appropriate measures. But not having is not a moral or charitable act towards other species. It is by seeking to have that species learn their limits and learn what not to have. Their allotment is determined by these interactions, and when a species doesn't fight to have, another will reduce its not have and take possession of whatever was abandoned. But in addition to these natural interactions, there are principles inherent to each species and its own evolution. The quest to have is a principle of life but so is satiety. Limits are external as well as internal.

In human beings, consciousness generates external and internal limits as well as relational limits. That's why existence is a balance between having and not having for all other species and lives without consciousness, but for humans, it is a question in its different dimensions. Ambivalence, doubt, and paradox are relational expressions of interactions between the individual and the world peculiar to human beings.

"What's mine is yours and yours is yours" seems like the antithesis of life, and only for beings with consciousness is it not. How can we understand life as something to be experienced while forfeiting what is ours? To understand it this way, a life must recognize that its vitality lies no longer in the tree itself but in the seed that falls from it. The fact that trees offer up their seed-rich fruit is a spiritual act. As an amazing example of "what's mine is yours and what's yours is yours," this act illustrates how forfeiting can affirm possession. Until now defined by our body's own experience, life transfers its experience of being to its fruit, and a new birth-delivery takes place—the delivery of self. Many people resist this birth, trying to escape it through attachment to their self or through proposals like euthanasia. Both attitudes are kinds of resistance to this birth; they are ways of having that try to elude paradox, a paradox in which "I am" more and more through that which "I don't have," while my possessing is primarily defined through that which I give away and do not take.

Birth as a delivery, as a handing over, is in itself a paradox. Every time there is a birth, a letting go, there is a discontinuity that feels completely absurd. It's simply that possession of life and our identity will be greatly expressed by not being. In order to hold no debts to its being, every living being will have to honor not being and accept the fact that its continuity can only be achieved through its disappearance. The experience of being has always embraced this "paradox" as its most profound question. The evolution from query (*frague*) to ambivalence (*shaila*), doubt (*kashia*), and paradox (*teiku*) is the natural tendency of a consciousness constantly exposed to the experience of being and not being.

From this perspective, "what's mine is yours" does not represent a form of renunciation but possession per se. It is a way of embracing death and its values in the midst of life itself.

The only thing we can possess at the end of our old age is whatever we don't have. Yet this has always been true, at every single moment. When we say we are defined by what we have and what we don't have, we are recognizing that in all phases of our lives, not having produced experiences of being. The mine that becomes yours is capable of producing as much experience of being as the obvious possession found in "what's mine is mine."

Throughout all its phases, life is a potential, or project, and this means it is defined by what is possible as well as by its limits. Not having always defines us as much as having, even if we tend to focus on having as the driving force of life. That is why everything that is good has a measure, or size. Without limits, nothing can be experienced as wellbeing. Our experiences with overabundance teach us this, for nothing is good when you get too much of it. Not even our state of health, which ensures our organism's survival, can exist independent from the project of life. The nature imbedded within our structure is responsible for our feeling of wellbeing, and not even health can be an absolute value. Old age involves a renunciation, and we try to make this period as good as it can be, to live it as well as we can, optimizing both our desires for longevity and for renunciation. This requires an artistic weaving of these two demands from our structural design, so as to ensure our best interests. The paradox occurs because we must take responsibility for the interests of a being that intrinsically, in addition to being, will have to forfeit its self. If we make having an absolute value by endlessly striving to possess, or make not having an absolute value by endlessly forfeiting, life loses its muscle tone and our experience of being grows flaccid. In other words, it is not possible to be without this constant balancing act between having and not having.

An enduring being—perhaps eventually enduring forever, if idealized visions of scientific progress prove true—would lose its ability to be because this experience is a relationship of balance between having and not having. Having one's self entirely and forever is the antithesis of the project implanted in us, and this project is what determines our being. Consciousness identifies this project as the need to explore "queries, ambivalences, doubts, and paradoxes," and it seems paradoxical to us that life's greatest drive is not its project—that being is merely a tool which can never substitute for the project itself.

Shakespeare's poetic and philosophical contribution is that being is not a commandment, or a fate, but a question. It seems paradoxical to us that "not to be" is a choice that qualifies existence just as much as "to be" does. The beauty of a paradox is that it isn't meant to be resolved, unlike queries, ambivalences, and doubts. A paradox is embraced or not. Its question is rhetorical, meant simply to keep the door open on an inquiry, without closing it with a question mark at the end. This is why the rabbis' time-honored use of a paradox to address questions that cannot be settled in the present—that is, *teiku*—translates this realm so well. In the rabbinic discussions of the Talmud, whenever an impasse was reached, a *teiku* was declared—somewhat like throwing in the towel, or calling investigations to a halt until some time in the future when new arguments or evidence may settle the impasse and allow a solution to be reached. The word itself is an initialization of the Hebrew words *Tishbi Itrats Kushiot U-beaiot*, which means "*Tishbi* [the prophet Elias] will clarify questions and paradoxes in the future." But perhaps more than a reference to the future, the prophet Elias serves as a mythical image of constant presence, as if the paradox were a query whose answer can never be found in the present. It is an answer that we can subtlety glimpse in the present, but this answer will never actually exist in the present. Forever and always, what is yet to come will understand the "question" embedded in this paradox better than the present itself. This kind of eternal query, which points to a possible answer that will never be found, lends the spiritual world its unique nature. The profound questions of the spirit are always paradoxical in essence.

Chapter V

The Economics of Desire

It is within the "spiritual" realm, where "what's mine is yours," that we better understand what a "thing" is. Every object of possession acquires the form of a "thing," and these things that we will have and we will not have eventually come to define our very being. These "things" are perceived in different ways in each of the four worlds: physical, emotional, intellectual, and spiritual. In their various manifestations, "things" lend the "question" peculiar to each of these realms its own particular hue.

Actually, things are not merely objects; they can take the form of ideas or even passions. All of our desires turn objects, people, possibilities, and pathways into things, and this is how they exist in our consciousness. In other words, they are not really things, or inanimate objects, but represent relationships between object and individual. Through their relation to an individual, these things define values and afford us an understanding of what the "other" is. Using spirituality, or radical humanism, Martin Buber tried to explain this basic act of existence, which transforms I-It relations into I-You relations. This ongoing production of conscious life frees us from the loneliness of being just one more thing in the Universe. And this is the paradoxical role played by death. Death gives us the chance "to be" precisely because it makes us confront the reality of "not being." Death is the steadfast landmark that puts us in a position of relationship—"being" up against "not being"—and lets us experience a universe beyond things; it allows us the strange perception that we are an entity, a subject. Understood as an organism, this entity has access to an identity, which in turn makes possession feasible. Nothing could be possessed if it were not for the "I," for being. Death is therefore our only escape from being just one more thing, one more It.

Possessing is actually a complete illusion, but at the same time it forms the most basic structure of our perceptions. The more illusory our experience, the more tangible, revealed, and immediate it becomes. Mystics believe that the more hidden something is, the more authentic it is; the more revealed, the closer it is to real and farther removed from the essence.

This is our question (our paradox) because in order for us "to have"—the fundamental yet momentary cornerstone of our experience of existence—we must likewise face the possibility of "not having." If "having" stands alone and is not part of an ongoing dialectical relationship with "not having," instead of fostering the experience of "being," it renders it unviable. This is what triggers today's complaints about the emptiness of consumerism. Consumption takes life's basic action—having—as an absolute value rather than as one dimension of a "question's" four dimensions. The utterly indispensable act of possessing is always a question that opens us up to choices, decisions, and, ultimately, life. If we really see what we possess, we can understand our choices about what we don't have, and this is the source of our identity.

A dear friend told me that on one of her trips to the East, she met a wise monk. She especially cherished one of his teachings. The monk often mentioned a pitcher that had belonged to his family, a pitcher that fascinated him. One day he invited her to his monastery where he kept it so she could see this small wonder for herself. After a long, grueling walk, she found herself looking at the object. The monk said, "Isn't it wonderful?" There was a pitcher in front of her. There was nothing very special about this object that brought a sparkle to the monk's eyes and stretched his lips into a rapt, enigmatic smile. Out of politeness, she pretended to be as much in awe of the pitcher as the monk was, keeping her unease to herself.

Many years later, after surviving a serious illness, she told me she understood what the monk had been talking about. There are "things," but when our eyes are awakened, we understand that things are not just things. Within them lies the "I," the relationship through which we place ourselves in the world and in existence. The true "thing" is all that this thing is, plus the sum of all that it "is not." The essence of any thing is how it reflects our existence. If we want to embrace pitchers, or any other object, with an attachment that lets us "have" without "not having," then we transform the sacred act of possession, of relationship between I and others, into a kiss that touches the void and hollowness of existence.

True things invite us to have them and to not have them. This is why "what's mine is yours" is so often just as powerful an act of possession as the childish pleasure of "yours is mine." There is just as much possession in one as the other. If you don't understand these two possibilities, you will quickly destroy the beauty and potential of possession itself, elevating it to a category above "question." And nothing is more questionable than "having." Having, without the "question," drains pitchers of their fascination and leaves them less capable of instilling wonder.

No matter how amazing vessels may be on the outside, they will only succeed in producing the breath of emptiness and meaninglessness. The depression assailing our world today is a reflection of the great number of possessions and acts of possession bereft of "questions."

WHAT WE HAVE IS WHAT WE GIVE AWAY

The spiritual dimension is not the apex of the experience of existence. Rather, it is the dimension that serves as a framework and lends balance to all other dimensions of existence. So it is not hierarchical, contrary to the impression we are given by the world of morality and religion and also by civilization itself. There's no denying that this dimension demands profound insight on our part if our human sensibilities are to perceive it as indispensable. It is at this most literal level that we discover that the potential for possession lies not only in what we may have but in what we don't have. If you live your life only from the perspective of what the world can offer in terms of "mine is mine and yours is mine," you are poor and live a half-hearted, meager existence.

If you experience all these dimensions and also recognize "having" in that which you "don't have," in that which you forfeit, and yet you return fully conscious of exercising possession, then you are a potent "being." But it is also essential to understand that this is not an ideal to be reached or a definitive answer to the questions of having. Whoever wants "to not have" in absolute terms is just as sick as a consumer who wants "to have" in absolute terms. "To Have or Not to Have" is an ongoing question, a sacred relationship in itself. Whoever wants to be "good" and possess only what he doesn't have, what he "gives away," is as materialistic and empty as his opposite. These are two different ways of trying to erase the question, with its accompanying ambivalences, doubts, and paradoxes. The egoist and the altruist possess very little.

Pitchers are only captivating if we experience the tension between "having" and "not having." Any other approach leaves our "being" flaccid, deprived of its self. This "question" must remain on the table until the very last moment of our lives. True, among the things we are most able to "have" are the things we give up and give away to others. But there's no formula; it's all about having the sensitivity to know how to use all the opportunities "to have" that life throws our way.

The Rabbi of Kotzk provides a fine example of this insight. When the rabbi was very ill, his son brought his own child to visit his grandfather. The father suggested the little boy pray for his grandfather's recovery. But the child came right out and said he'd only do so if the elderly man would give him his wristwatch. The father was about to reprimand his son for such selfish behavior when the rabbi stopped him. He said, "I'd rather he'd pray because of this watch than based on convention or morality."

It is clear to the rabbi that the meaning of our acts does not lie at one pole or another. For a child, there is nothing more appropriate than "yours is mine." When the rabbi gave his grandson his watch, it was a much more powerful way of propelling the forces of life forward than making the boy responds with an insight he didn't have. This is why it is vital that we don't oversimplify these teachings, because we can possess something by forfeiting and not having it, but of course we can also possess by simply "having."

In a universe where possession only exists through the interaction between a being and the world around it—where possession is essentially an illusion—expanding possession will always depend upon our questions. For us to attain as many possessions as possible, as we endeavor to imbue our being with an essence, we surrender ourselves to the sacred task of "having" or forsaking "having." Thus we let queries, ambivalences, doubts, and paradoxes reinforce our experience of "being" and endow us with an identity.

Herein lies the amazing wonder of possession: insofar as it is an illusion, it is also infinite. This is why we can compete over "having" but not over possession. Possession will always be individual and non-transferable; no one can take it from the being that produced it, or deprive him of it. But to think of it as an absolute essence, as a thing dissociated from a being, is as absurd as thinking of it as finite. The more you realize possession is tied to your very existence, the more you will possess. Infinite and non-transferable, possession is the most concrete of all human experiences, even if its essence is—as we said—a mere impression, an illusionary aftereffect of desire. And if you think this seems like a paradox, or something ludicrous, you're right—that's just what it is. It is an absurdity that is fundamental and necessary to the experiences of "being" and of "having."

WHAT YOU CAN HAVE

These reflections help us understand that although possession is an illusion or trick that allows us to experience "being," it is central to consciousness. "What is my size? What belongs to me and what doesn't?" are existential questions. They tell us that what permits possession is "being" and its awareness of its own existence. What possesses is the "I," while concomitantly the "I" is built out of possessions. The wellbeing of an "I" will always depend on what it "has" and what it "doesn't have." Assured of what it has, the "I" becomes fuller; on the other hand, assured of what it doesn't have, the "I" can prevent its own bloating. If the "I" is not full, it suffers malnourishment; if it feels bloated, it becomes sick to its stomach.

What you can have depends upon your "I"—on what it has room for and what it appropriates. Any possession not befitting a given "I" will be false, and this is something we recognize. Whether we're talking about the material or the emotional realm, if something doesn't "belong" to the I, sooner or later it will be lost or betrayed.

We do our best to avoid the experience of being "dispossessed" because it is the opposite feeling of "being" and because it represents the deconstruction of our being. These experiences are quite apparent in each of the realms discussed earlier. In the physical realm, they are about the harsh experience of losing; in the emotional realm, they are about the experience of betrayal or injustice; in the intellectual realm, they are about the sense of worthlessness that comes when we feel weakened or stagnant; and in the spiritual realm, they find expression in depression, which makes us forget the sacred element contained within the act of "being." All such experiences are expressions of an "I" that cannot possess, because possession will always depend primarily on an "I" that can encompass possession and embrace the experience of appropriating itself. Only when we possess ourselves can we avail ourselves of possessions in order to build and affirm our selves. We've seen how this resembles a paradox. What comes first: the chicken or the egg, the sense of oneself or the possibility of possession?

Back in the first century, the wise Hillel stated that a sense of self was essential if possession was not to be destructive and work against being itself. These words from *Ethics of the Fathers* have been attributed to him:

> If I am not for me, who will be for me?
> (*Im ani li, mi li?*)

> And if I am for me, what am I?
> (*U-ke-she-ani lê-atsmi, ma ani?*)

> And if not now, when?
> (*Vê-im ein ló achshav, ematai?*)

His aphorism is constructed around the notion of possession. If "not for me," for whom? If I do not take possession of my "I," who will? Playing with the words "void" (*ain*) and "I" (*ani*), Hillel underscores the similarity between "I" and "NOTHINGNESS" as recognized by the mystics. Without possession, the "I" is "NOTHINGNESS." And who will take possession of my self, if not myself?

But once I have taken possession of me, how can I know the dimensions and stature of this "I"? This can only be accomplished by possessing things in this world and by knowing our ability to have and the grandeur of not having. This is a lifelong task, in which we endlessly possess and dispossess in the effort to determine "what we are." And only then, in possession of our selves and open to possessions and to renunciations that are likewise possessions, do we find ourselves facing the act of attaining the here and now. This act of possessing the here and now is what we call "being." As stated earlier, "being" is filled with "having." Having my self makes it possible "to have what is mine" and paves the way for "having what is yours." Of course, very often "having yours" may mean "not having," which is also a form of possession. Therefore, possession is what reinforces the experience of "being," whether by choosing to have or by choosing to not have.

We often think that the things we "don't have" are nobler or greater, precisely because morality compels us to see them as things to be "taken from this world." The expression "you can't take it with you" makes us believe that in moral terms "not having" is an asset with greater liquidity than "having" when we leave this world. Later on, we will see this isn't true. What matters most is true possession, and whenever we have something but would have more if we didn't have it, or whenever we don't have something but would have more if we had it, we are going against possession. As a result, we weaken our sense of what we are, and if we persist in this serious error, we eventually lose possession of ourselves. And who will take possession of our selves, if not ourselves?

We can only have that which affirms our sense of self. The illusion of possession feeds the illusion of "I," and we can only build the indispensable experience of being out of this entanglement of illusions. Every experience of being thus lies in the query, ambivalence, doubt, and paradox of "having or not having"—for "being" means honoring our sensibilities, reduced to the physical, emotional, intellectual, and spiritual realms. If you always honor your decisions about what to have and what not to have within these realms, you will attain the here and "now." Is this "here" the opposite of "when"? "Now" has substance and is the greatest possession, a possession we do indeed "take with us" when we leave this world. But "when?" is the opposite of possession; it is a potential that has not been seized or taken possession of. A life comprised of "when?" does not have an "I" (*ani*) and resembles "NOTHINGNESS" (*ain*).

MANNA—POSSESSING NOTHINGNESS

We have seen that what enables us to possess is the appropriateness of what we get and what we give up. The more we seek to have, dissociated from the question of "having or not having," the less we possess. The pillars of possession are grounded in the "I": the stronger it is, the greater its ability to possess. From now on, we will understand possession as the potential we gain from the act of taking possession of something or giving it up.

A special symbol of possession is biblical manna, the miraculous sustenance provided to the Hebrews every day in the desert. Available at the break of each morning, this substance enlightens our understanding of possession on the spiritual plane. Manna means "allotment" or measure. As a principle, you could only gather as much manna as you would consume that same day. If the amount you took did not serve your true needs alone, or if you used it for purposes other than bodily nourishment, the surplus would decay and even jeopardize your daily allotment. If you tried to claim manna for a week, a month, a year, or a whole lifetime, you would pay the price of not knowing the limits of what suffices, and in this place with no limits, there can be no real possession because there is no "I" capable of containing possessions within itself.

When the recipient of the manna is not the "I", but rather the impulse to have grounded in fear and insecurity, then all manna is at risk. This is why the commentators said manna tasted different to everyone who ate it. Manna has no distinct flavor; instead, each "I" has its own unique way of savoring it. The taste of every "I" is the interaction between the outside and the inside; it is a relationship, a balance that makes things either delicious or inedible. And we experience the most horrible of all tastes when we have no taste for anything, when our palate no longer senses anything because we fail to connect supply and demand appropriately. Unless something is appropriate, we cannot appropriate or possess it. There is a symbolic relation between taste and possession, for both constitute a precise measure, a certain quality that is the product of an accurate proportion. By finding this proportion, things can become part of other things and be possessed; yet it is not the subject that possesses but rather the precise ratio between need and supply. How much someone wants and how much someone else doesn't want affirms individuality and the identity of things, while strengthening our perception of existence.

Perhaps this is in part how we resolve the paradox, since it demonstrates why "not having" is essential to the experience of being. A thing will always be an "It" until it can find other "things" with which to bond in order to meet a need. Things that bond with other things in appropriate fashion possess each other and reinforce "being." This interdependence is manna, an allotment whose quantity represents a specific quality that cannot be substituted by any other quantity. The specificity of demands and their legitimacy permit possession, which is the illusory, momentary act of having or not having that can fill our moments with meaning and a sense of existence.

What is most amazing is that manna is described as something almost ethereal, lacking its own essence. The sustenance provided by manna does not come from its substance but from its appropriateness, from its correct measure. Possession is the taste for life. If you cannot possess, you lose your taste for the things of this world. For when things possess and are possessed, they award us taste for what exists. Through possession we gain our awareness of these myriad flavors and palates, as vast as the things that exist in the universe. So we come to understand that possession is a measure, just like manna. And the essence of manna is Nothingness (*ain*), which is the fabric from which *ani*—the "I"—is woven.

Our civilization's most common mistake is believing that possession is an absolute condition (a reality) and that things can be taken possession of by other things. What is lost here is the understanding that possession is instead a measure for the bonding between things. This mistaken form of possession does not strengthen our experience of being but attacks and impoverishes it instead. The persistent quest for many erroneous possessions eventually induces the "I" to see itself as "Nothingness."

Instead of sustaining "being," this type of possession consumes it. Whatever is inordinate and inappropriate (i.e., cannot be appropriated) not only corrodes all acts of possession, but jeopardizes them as well, especially the possession of one's self.

In the end, the harder you try to hold onto something to make sure you have it, the more ephemeral this experience will be, eventually showing you how much you don't have. Holding on tightly or loosely enough is essential to "being." It is this appropriate tonus that allows me to be for myself; that is, that allows what I am to manifest itself at a certain moment and take possession of "now."

YOU CAN TAKE A LOT WITH YOU

The idea that you can't take anything with you to the grave is very often understood to be a moral statement that deems possession and attachment negative. But it's not quite like that. It would be very simple if we could act positively just by forfeiting things and battling any type of greed. Yet balance does not depend solely on one of its poles. Harmony is always a healthy relationship between different and, almost always, opposing forces. The essence of this opposition is not how we tend to think of it. Duality is a resource through which we experience things better; as real and palpable as these oppositions may seem to us, they are aspects of one same thing.

It's true that the baggage we're allowed to take with us on our final life journey doesn't include even the smallest carry-on, but we can still take a lot with us and we should. No one can take our true possessions away from us. They will remain forever embedded in our very identity, woven from the small acts of possession in which we engage throughout our lives. These acts include moments when we guarantee that "mine is mine" and, sometimes, that "yours is mine." Winning always involves an invasion, when a "yours becomes mine." And there's something healthy about this. No balance can exclude the most basic, childish act of possession. In

82

this realm, possession achieves balance when I discover that by constantly winning, I may lose myself, my own identity. There is a kind of winning that doesn't involve yours but rather mine. When I win like this, "mine is yours." When I win like this, the challenge is not the other, but my own impulse. The impulse that ensures my continual survival is the same one that can make me sick or make me hurt myself.

We can understand this if we look at our own immune system. Everything that can be defended, and therefore attacked, can only work properly within the parameters of balance. Any inordinate act of defense, like any inordinate act of winning, is an assault on the principles of balance. Thus many illnesses—like those that leave us vulnerable to outside attack by viruses or bacteria—find their roots in allergies, inflammations, or immunological disorders brought on by our own bodies. In my zeal to guarantee that "mine is mine," I may end up doing the opposite, causing a shift in balance towards "what is mine is no longer mine."

Possession is the product of balance. We can only possess that which we can allow ourselves "to not have" when it is available in abundance, or that which we legitimately take possession of when it is lacking. Possession is therefore an art. And everything that we truly possess accompanies us from this life because it is life itself. We actually take possession of the here and now's that life affords us. Whenever we live without bearing in mind the constant question of "having or not having" we lose the chance to take possession of that particular moment's "here and now."

Whenever we take possession of our here and now, whether we have or do not have, we carry this possession away with us forever. Moments like this resonate; they are not lost in a fading past. Instead, each moment we live as a here and now becomes a permanent fixture of our existence, one that we carry wherever we go. For we are the sum of such moments, and what we are given to possess is not an immaterial, imaginary "I" but the path of our presence, recorded in the tracks of the here and now's we have possessed. We take all this with us because this is what we are.

We take with us whatever we have deliberately decided not to have as well as what we have legitimately taken for ourselves. What we cannot take with us are the unnecessary things we amass—an undeniable record of missed opportunities to take possession of other real things that can be possessed in this world. Nor do we take with us those things we failed to take possession of, things that could have belonged to us but that we forfeited for reasons having nothing to do with a decision between "having or not having." Whenever we give up or forfeit something without filtering it through our queries, ambivalences, doubts, and paradoxes, we miss out on the chance to possess what we "do not have." And not having without possessing is as big a waste as having without possessing.

Yes, you can take a lot with you from this world. And it is the duty of whomever lives fully to accumulate a multitude of true possessions that can be exchanged for any other currency, possessions boasting a liquidity that resists the loss of life itself. Because a life possessed is something no one can wrench away from your "I." This is our immortality, derived from an "I" that at times is just an illusion or trick, but that by conquering here and nows becomes a true identity —and we become possessed by ourselves. And then what we take with us is our very selves, embedded in everything we feel as ourselves, had or not had. Here is my true "I," the essence of my undeniable existence, inalienable from my self.

Enjoying squatter's rights over my self for a certain period of time shows that an illegitimate, invented "I" becomes not only a recognized possession but also stays on for the enjoyment of anyone, even after I depart this life. Because when we truly possess, we not only take it with us; we also leave the world a legacy that can be possessed and enjoyed by those who lend us our continuity. From Nothingness, the "I" becomes an "it" that we can relate to even when we are no longer present.

After all, presence means taking possession of the here and now, and it is not temporal but atemporal in nature. Each and every single "here and now" that we take hold of becomes our property, appropriated and forever uniting one thing with other things within time. This unique integration will forever resonate among things and will be the source of many other acts of possession and many other "I's" built through appropriation—through the appropriate relation between things.

QUALITY OF LIFE AND THEFT

Although possession occurs between things, it is never about the possession of things. Possession is about the relationship between things that we build through our questions about "having or not having." There are those who have but who really do not have. There are those who do not have but really have. And, of course, there are those who do not have and really do not have, just as there are those who have and really have.

Possession only exists for those who "have and really have" or for those who "do not have and really have." These two forms of possession create relationships between the "I" and all other things—and they are the essence of our existence.

Reb Nachman, from whom we drew a number of earlier teachings, has a rather interesting view of possession. He challenges those who believe they enjoy a good quality of life to take a litmus test to measure just how authentic this quality is. He suggests that people who think they benefit from a good quality of life imagine losing the things they have one by one. If the quality of their lives also diminishes as the number of things does, then they do not really have a good quality of life.

Perhaps people enjoy "quantity of life" but lack "quality," which is measured by a person's true possessions, by what he has and deliberately does not have. No one can be deprived of quality of life, since it consists of acts of possession—and these acts of possession are inalienable. Things may indeed be taken or even stolen from us but our relationship to things is something no one can steal. These things belong to the "I," which is non-transferable in its relationship to things.

At the same time, whoever steals has but does not have possession. There is no room in a thief's "I" for possession of the stolen goods. Whoever steals has less "I," that is, less possession of himself. This kind of "having," which diminishes possession, runs counter to quality of life, because the act of being surrounded by many things while not possessing them is a great curse. We can't take the things of this world with us, but we can take our possessions. And the more we have without possessing means we were unable to produce here and now's during the course of our existence. And the less we possess of the here and now, the less we will know our size or "what we are." And the less clearly defined our dimensions and magnitudes, the less authentic our "I" and the less possession we have of our selves.

Nothingness and "I" are the poles that express our experience of "existing" and of being. We must be ever attentive to this, because their content is represented by the acts of possession we achieve throughout life.

True quality of life is a victory that can be measured by our identity itself. The possibility that we might lose this quality is proof that we never had it in the first place.

It's impossible to steal a true possession. Theft is a state that actually represents an economic interaction. Seen from a radical angle, both sides are ultimately involved in this economic interaction. If we imagine a thief offering the car owner a penny for the vehicle he's about to steal, the owner would see this as a good deal under the terms of this specific interaction, since it might be the only way of saving his life. This indeed falls within the realm of value. For example, no one would work for a paltry sum like the minimum wage if this didn't beat the alternative of starving to death.

Both thief and victim are involved in an interaction about the custody of something that hasn't been in the thief's hands until that moment, but at no point is there any change within the realm of possession. The proof of this is that the thief will soon turn the object into money, the great "washer" of things people have but do not possess.

Moral judgments aside, anything that cannot be possessed has little or no value. All robberies, whether the work of professional thieves or of people engaged in routine interactions, deconstruct the perpetrator's "I" and leave him more vulnerable to not taking anything with him from this world.

This is why much of our envy and feelings of dissatisfaction have nothing to do with true needs but with our keen interest in what others possess. Yet if we are allowed to have these coveted things, we still will not achieve wellbeing. For having custody of things does not reproduce the wealth of possessing them. An envious person knows this, and therefore doesn't want what the other has. Taking what the other has is what a jealous person really wants, but an envious individual only wants to keep the other from possessing, since he who envies finds himself in the position of a thief.

Theft is an obstacle to possession. Stealing intensifies our sensation that things can be taken from us. On the one hand, it reinforces our illusion that "custody" of things can replace our interaction with them. On the other, it also reinforces our sense of insecurity. The only people who actually steal are the ones who believe that by taking something they achieve possession of it. What happens is just the opposite; this attitude deprives us of the possibility of possession. So riches that are not possessed but only remain in our custody do not bring us any pleasure; instead, we are tortured by the thought of losing them. Quite likely this is what we most often feel about money: the pleasure of having it is much less than the suffering caused by not having it.

Everything we experience in this way is not possessed. The things we possess bring us pleasure and a sense of self. These are the things it is better to have than to not have; after all, possessing is precisely about interaction, decisions, and life exercised in the act of deciding whether "to have or not to have." If our choice is to have, "not having" can never represent a more intense experience than "having." In possession, "not having" also stems from a choice and therefore does not induce the fear of loss.

Possession does not encompass loss. Anything that can be lost does not belong to our set of possessions. Even a "thing" that once was mine and that I once possessed but that is no longer available to me is still a possession. It is a possession of the kind "what is mine is yours and what is yours is yours." Because it was something of mine that raised queries, ambivalences, doubts, and paradoxes, it became a possession. In other words, whatever its state of "custody" at the moment, I still hold it—no longer in the form of "having" but in the form of "being."

This is what possession makes possible: the definitive conversion of what we have into what we are. It is a means of interaction between the "I" and the world, between I and You.

This is the big difference between Property and Possession, a difference that only the spiritual realm can reveal to us sharply.

PROPERTY WITHOUT POSSESSION—
HOW TO HAVE WITHOUT BEING?

The spiritual universe speaks directly to the experience of maturing and growing old. Human beings experience life as a commodatum, that is, something on loan to us for free. The biggest impact of having a consciousness is that we perceive life as something that grants us rights for a period not to exceed one hundred twenty years. This perception affects how we value everything in the world around us. And as with any temporary contract, the value of things declines over time. When we pay for a commercial spot's goodwill, it will be worth a lot at the beginning of our lease but less and less as it draws to a close.

So it is that as our life goes by, "things" tend to be worth less. This is a vital experience because it reveals nuances of "being" and "having" that are obfuscated by the exponential value youth attaches to "things." Young people's attachment to "things" is legitimate, since an object's usefulness makes it easy to confuse it with the experience of "being." So property is confused with possession. Since having property seems to mean we can use the property for so long it seems like forever, we assume we have possession of it. A mature person often finds it rather pathetic when a young person acts smug about property he or she believes to constitute possession. Only our consciousness of life's finitude puts our property to the test of whether or not it constitutes possession. If it does, we can take it with us, and its value will not diminish as the commodatum of life approaches its end.

What we are talking about here has direct implications on wealth. Wealth doesn't have anything to do with how much we have but what we possess. "Having" is about property, while "having or not having" is about possession. The first is about holding onto and having custody of something; the second is about the interaction between an individual and the use of things. So possession is tied to use and to value. A rich man is not someone who has things but someone who makes use of things. The more someone has use for the things available to him, the richer he is.

People who have access to fortunes they can never use in this lifetime hold wonderful property, but how much they possess is another matter altogether. We don't know how much a magnate possesses; we only know what he owns. Everything he owns is liable to no longer being. Through theft, bad investments, wasteful spending, poor management, or death, property changes hands. No thing is under anyone's eternal ownership, because things cannot be the eternal property of some other thing. But possession is something else. Possession means you have a monopoly over what existed and interacted with the world around it. The subject is no longer an "It" but an "I," that is, a construct of interactions between things. These interactions transcend the reality of things and free them from the limits of their very nature. A human being's transcendence is linked to the possibility of no longer being a mere thing in this universe. To borrow Buber's language, I-It is the perception experienced by a "thing" with a consciousness. On the other hand, I-You represents the experience of transcendence that can be enjoyed by a thing with consciousness.

Thus, possessions have to do with living and with a person's interactions during the course of his life. Possession is a product of existence and the materiality of existence.

We each know how much we possess. There are no manuals and no recipes. You can possess a lot, living a life grounded on leisure and friendships or on dedication to a cause. You can possess just as much if you have only a little property or a lot of property. There are magnates who build their lives and their fortunes while engaged in profound interaction with the world, and they possess much. There are poor people who protect themselves from risk and from effort, and they possess little. There are magnates who will take little or nothing from this world, and the dispossessed who have enviable amounts of possessions and will take a lot with them.

As time passes, we learn to distinguish the concept of property from the concept of possession. Believing at first that we are eternal and immortal, we go from a sense of "having" that merges property and possession to a sense of "having" that faces the finitude of life and therefore sees the contrast between property and possession. Vital "questions" about having thus come out into the open. Young people must have the wisdom to learn how to curb their instinct for property and temper it through investment in possessions. It's important for them to be aware of the paradoxes of "having or not having" and not just the "questions."

The experiences of "having" and "being" reinforce each other. Only through wisdom and appropriateness (questions) can "having" turn into possession. And we can only achieve possession if we have room for it within our being. Anything that doesn't fit inside our being, anything that consists of holding on to things or placing priority on one set of things over another—rather than expressing an interaction between things—will not afford us possession. How much of our assets we possess is directly tied to our experience of wellbeing and of being.

Therefore, property does not have a neutral relationship to possession. The greater our property, the greater our possession will have to be, if it is to represent an experience that strengthens "being." So it is not worth having more property if we can't possess it. Food serves as a good illustration. When I satisfy my hunger, I take possession of the food I eat. If I appropriate more food than I am able to possess, it will have a negative impact on my health and wellbeing.

The limits of possession are not a moral issue; they lie in "being." The more you can use your assets to reinforce your experience of being, the better. But any excess that cannot be contained within being is the opposite of possession—it is a "having" that diminishes existence.

In order to have, I need to be, and in order to be, I need to have. Do not lose sight of this relationship. Have nothing that does not fit within your being; have nothing that you do not possess. Likewise, do not feel anything you do not have and that is not grounded on the conquest of possessions, either through having or through not having.

NOT HAVING AND DESIRE

Not to have is the beginning of desire.
— Wallace Stevens

Possession is built from the relationship between having and not having. Contrary to what we might think, possession is far removed from controlling, clutching, or monopolizing. Whenever we try to exercise this kind of hold over things, we end up having without also possessing. It's not unusual that someone who gets what he really wanted will afterward ask himself in surprise, "Where'd my desire go?" By itself, having cannot yield the same quality of wellbeing as the potential to have. It is right here in this place of not having that all passions occur, and it is also from this place that the big paradox between the I and the things of this world emerges, whether these things are objects or people. The place of desire and of possession as well is located in not having. This not having is infused with questions about having or not having. The sensitive and the wise understand the mystery of persevering in not having, and they strive to remain on this edge of life as long as possible, curbing their impulse to have. Although it is the goal of possession, having never takes place within its realm; in fact, possession almost always comes undone with the act of having. This doesn't mean we can't have something as part of our efforts to accomplish our endeavors, but the pleasure of having is always dependent upon the echo of absence and need within our memories. Children suffer from this experience more than any other group. Their desire to have is so absolute that we are amazed when they lose their interest for a highly coveted object once they get it. Is it just that the novelty and newness wears off, abandoning the object once obtained? It's not that simple. The act of having really corrodes desire because of our relationship of control towards things. If the possibility of not having were still there, our interest would not wane.

Possession has to do with relationships between the inside and outside. It is this relationship more than the object of our desire that affords us the possibility of being and underlies our desire to possess. We think possession will make the desired object part of our selves and that this will strengthen our being, but as we have seen, the experience of existence and identity only takes place within the sphere of relationships. Lovers and couples go through this all the time. At some moment between dating and getting married, we often trade possession for having. Madly in love with his girlfriend, the besotted suitor already possesses, but as soon as his girlfriend becomes "his"—as soon as he "has" her— his passion disappears. Having cannot sustain the relationship because having always implies invalidating the other. The other can only be independent as long as it is possible to not "belong to," to not be "had." Sexual intimacy is thus a way of constantly preserving distance and, above all, not allowing the other "to have" us. This is a remarkable aspect of not having, one enjoyed only by those courageous enough to embrace insecurity and risk fear. Not having always represents the risk of death, of becoming undone, of absence of self, and of losing one's soul. As if moments, life, and being itself could be captured and cloistered in order to guarantee our experience of being. This experience cannot be clutched in our hands, nor can it be frozen or made static.

Materiality is about the trouble we have coming to terms with this. If the food I eat becomes part of my body and if what I take as my property becomes exclusively mine, it seems to me that having should provide for my being. These experiences reinforce our belief that the road to possession is having. But possession always mimics the lover's dilemma.

Written in the language of lovers pining for each other, the book Song of Songs portrays the soul's longing for the sacred. In it, we read:

"I was asleep, but my heart was wakeful. Hark, my BELOVED knocks!"

Being asleep represents foolish passivity and a numbing absence that keeps me from hearing what my heart hears: someone's knocking at the door. It's not just anyone who's knocking; it's the incredible opportunity to be. It is "being" that constantly knocks at our door, seductively inviting us to an encounter. "Being" complains that it is subject to exclusion, and it demands an ongoing relationship between the inside and outside. It isn't possible "to be" without this encounter at the door, at the threshold between our self and the other. Being is thus exiled from my deadened, numb body. "Let me in!" cries the possibility of being, as if enticing us to possess it.

But the beloved knows it is not so simple. He knows the risk of looking for excuses, like those we read in the Song of Songs: "I'm on my way, but first I have to get ready, I haven't put my perfume on yet, I've got to see to a few things before I can receive my beloved" is the beloved's reaction. Yet if he tarries in opening the door, he will discover his beloved has disappeared; he looks for her but doesn't find her. This tragic loss is unbearable; it is the antithesis of having. If, on the other hand, he rushes to the door and opens it too soon, instead of disappearing, his beloved will turn into a thing, an It, and in having her, he loses the chance for possession.

Tension between the inside and outside is essential, for here is where we experience existence. The knock at the door is the tension we cannot lose. We can't fall asleep and not hear it. Thanks to our hearts, this doesn't happen, but how can we ensure this encounter will take place, since we run the risk either of dawdling and letting the inside be devoured by the outside, or of precipitating ourselves and letting the outside be invaded by the inside?

Whoever chooses to not have may lose the object of his desire, which leaves. Whoever chooses to have may lose the chance for possession. To have or not to have is the question, just like the tension of the beloved knocking at our door! The sacred is elusive and cannot be captured by any act or guideline. Our ability to be alive—to be—has to do with hearing the knock at the door and maintaining the tension, which neither empties us out nor fills us up. This void that does not "have" and that refuses to "have" is where the experience of existence is found. It is as if we were shells or husks ready to hold whatever will fill us up, but this can never reward us with the magnificent experience of our empty space. This void is the promise of encounter; it is the door where inside and outside touch. It is the outside and its things that create the inside. It is the inside and its passion that create the outside.

What happens most often is that we miss this moment of possession. We ruin our chance for possession, either because we experience the void of reaching the door too late, or because we succumb to obsession and idolatry, impatiently rushing to the door.

When it comes to passion, no experience can ever replace the experience of our eyes, because it can hold within it both the void and the possibility of an encounter, without in either case dissolving the paradoxical tension that constitutes the sole place of possession. We're not talking about the possession of the other or of any thing, but the possession of our self.

CARESSING INSTEAD OF CLINGING

The same Song of Songs describes this moment of possession in the lover's enthusiastic words: *"Oh, give me of the kisses of your mouth, for your love is more delightful than wine."*

The opposite of being asleep is being drunk. This place of absence and of being empty of oneself is the setting for possession. Kisses and sweetness represent this state of being that we seek so madly and that is furtively revealed to us in erotic experience. Eros is the request to be filled, without explicitly specifying whether we want to be invaded or to invade, whether we want to be inside, possessing, or filled and possessed. The sensuousness of a kiss represents this portal between inside and outside, where I process the uncertainty of whether I have or am had by the other. At this point, the question "to have or not to have" becomes luminous and electric in its rush of presences, through which we participate in being not like a movie or reflection of our thought but like the instantaneous unleashing of "being here's" that lend us form and release an ocean of existence.

To kiss is to be at the door, reveling in the sweet possibility of opening the door or not. This wine can be compared to no other, because it frees us from the duality of existing in our selves or in the other, in the inside or the outside. It allows us to stop being prisoners of the I or the Other (of things), and know possession for an instant.

The world, however, is cruel to existence, constantly cheating it out of its essence by proposing to fill it with materiality, putting the dissolute choice of having above all else. As if having could make up for what is missing or absent. But existence is in itself a void, a hollow to be preserved.

So when it comes to possession, the appropriate gesture is not to hang on or cling to—gestures typical of having—but to caress. When we caress, it's as if we were searching for the void within the other and our hands do not want to grip but simply pay court to this vacuum, to what has been made empty. When our caresses are an effort to hold onto something, we lose possession and fall asleep, numbed by the experience of having something. Reminding us that our beloved is knocking at the door, only our hearts can wake us from this numbness that tries to hold and hang on to.

Whenever we manage to caress, a void remains in us forever. No one can rob us of the void that we touch and describe with our hands, using gestures that try to reproduce the boundaries of emptiness, of the void.

Our lives are made up of these moments when we caress, and we will only remember them. Even at the end of our lives, when it seems we no longer hold within us the possibility of enjoying the things of this world, whosoever has possessed during his lifetime will have his possessions forever. He will not live in loneliness, emptiness, or sadness. Possessions map out the relief of our souls and keep us from ever being abandoned by our selves. This is the ultimate gesture of whoever leaves this world. Unlike the baby who comes into the world trying to grab onto everything, now comes the effort to caress. Indifferent to things, our open hand tries to touch the void; we return to no-things, to the things we do not have.

This being filled with things it doesn't have always stands before its desire, the source of all possessions. The beautiful and the aesthetic, the pleasant and the pleasurable, the delectable and the soothing—all this is disposable compared to the wine of wines that is desire... just like the day, which has the courage to discard the lovely moonlit night in a caress that is the opposite of having and that permits the cosmic possession of its own void. This is what we perceive in the transitory nature of day and night, of the seasons, and of our own lives. It was probably this caress that permitted the Creation and caused it to make things manifest.

The experience of existence can be found at the threshold where things kiss, but this door—this boundary—is a place whose borders blur easily and voids are deformed. This blurring and deforming is the place where consumerism and fetishism numbs us. Our hearts call out to us: "Wake up, for someone's knocking at the door right now!"

I'M ONLY INTERESTED IN WHAT'S FOR FREE

How we understand value always involves our perception of supply and demand. If demand is great but supply scarce, value rises; if things are the other way around, value falls. Our markets are grounded in this perception, which is all about having. In our world, prices are determined by how hard it is to have. Yet can we imagine markets and relations where the key concern would be possession? That is, markets and relations where we would value presence and being instead of having? How much is "being" worth and what is the cost of "being"?

Markets grounded on being would have to place priority on the void and desire rather than on control and monopoly. They would have to offer something that had no price—not because the thing was priceless (the maximization of having) but because it represented the void. When something has no price but is not worthless, we say it is "for free."

In the world of having, we hear the echo of economist Milton Friedman: "There's no such thing as a free lunch!" In the market of having, nothing can be dissociated from a price. Desert manna would find no place on this menu that balances different wants and needs. But in the world of possession, few lunches in life are as special as those we receive gratis.

The very word "gratis" comes from the word "grace," which defines a relation of supply independent of any demand—a present. Economists would claim that such relations merely conceal subliminal prices and costs that will eventually become apparent. Yet as people live and mature, we often hear them declare: "I'm no longer interested in anything unless it's free!" What they mean is that the world of prices fails to encompass the values of reality, especially the values dearest to them.

The fact that non-utilitarian relationships are possible—relationships in which people caress existence rather than trying to clench it in their hands—makes possession possible. And nothing is more wonderful or magical than something we get for free, as an act of grace. Even if something free soon proves to be attached to demands and prices as well, we can still experience it for a moment. And we are captivated by the transcendence of such moments. The bulk of our most vivid memories, the ones that resonate within our souls, comprise this kind of experience.

The Eros that lies within the realm of what is gratis comes from a place that is neither inside or outside... this is what makes it erotic. Standing in the doorway, what is gratis seduces us. And before it is filled with prices and quotations, an emptiness imbued with value takes hold.

Fortunate is he who ventures out into the world each morning looking not for a good deal but to gather what is gratis. And the world is full of such opportunities.

Our streets overflow with them, but they are ignored. Like manna that drops from the heavens day after day after day, the world awakes with these presents. If we rush to harvest them, in our haste they will materialize into things we will have and thus will they be drained of their mystery. If we dally, they will rot, because what is free belongs to the moment; it is fleeting and cannot be stored away.

Knowing how to gather the dew of kindnesses and divine graces bestowed upon us by things and people is the fruit of paradise. This fruit represents the realm of things that come gratis. In playing its role, fruit hangs on the cusp between preserving its pit and offering itself up. Of all the foods, none is more delectable or aromatic than fruit. Nothing is more naïve and giving than fruit. It is the only food that does not depend upon anything's death to preserve someone else's life. It is without doubt nature's free lunch—given to us gratis. And our gathering ancestors knew this. They lived in a paradise that certainly presented fewer opportunities for acquiring things and boasted less abundance than the garden we dwell in, but they lived immersed in a market devoid of costs or prices, where having was not a way of experiencing being.

The forbidden fruit of paradise was Eros, at whose door our beloved knocks. Perhaps this explains a fruit that was forbidden yet available. If the Creator had not wanted humans to taste of this fruit, why tempt them with the possibility? The answer to this question lies in the question itself. Possession—the "not having" recommended by the Creator—would not be possible unless "having" were possible.

But Adam and Eve insist on having the fruit. They don't realize the fruit is already theirs; in fact, it was much more theirs, much more a possession, before they tried to grab it in their hands or savor it with their tongues. This gesture that seemed to be all about taking possession was about nothing but want and loss. With this bite, the world became permeated with prices. The future and tomorrow were made manifest when value came into being. Adam and Eve then knew worry—that is, they learned to fret over a situation before they even faced it. This anticipation allowed values to emerge, and with them, the notion of death. And death is the mother of all prices.

This paradise of gratis things is still with us, but it is guarded by Cherubims brandishing whirling swords; whoever dares pass through them must cast off his worry about tomorrow's sustenance and stop calculating how much each and every thing is worth in hopes he may have it; hardest of all, he must be able to stand "not having." The realm of what is free only becomes real for those who don't want to take it, for those who caress and respect its void.

Whoever experiences this kind of possession will strive to maintain voids and distances. Without possessing or being possessed, he will experience the only place where his moments in time and his self can be possessed—and these acts of possession are what grant us our true body, the essence of our existence.

"To be or not to be" or "to have or not to have" are not only the questions; they are existence and possession per se. Whoever knows how to overcome the trepidations and illusions that impel us to abandon this limbo will be and will have. In this void between being and not being, or between having and not having, lies all the grace, all that is gratis, in this world.

THE ECONOMICS OF DESIRE

"To have or not to have" endeavors to preserve desire itself. Desire lies at the core of all economics, encompassing everything necessary to our survival, and these needs guide our longing to have. But desire must always be greater than the demands that have been met. It stands for a measure that has to surpass whatever is available.

This is what drives a world of consumerism. If our desire must always be greater than what we "have," herein we find the root of greed and waste. For desire, the only thing that will ever suffice is "a little bit more." Although this understanding is accurate in quantitative terms, it is totally off the mark in qualitative terms. Desire is not sustained by "more" but by the void. The world—and perhaps even theDesire does not represent "more"; it is the "void." The world—and perhaps even the universe—cannot sustain the desire for "more" because this would require infinite resources. Yet this isn't the biggest problem. What is truly appalling is that "more" is not about desire. It is because of this common misunderstanding that Creation was dismantled as a setting for paradise, and our vision of hell was built. Desire is not insatiability. Insatiability is toxic to desire and is the source of our sorrows.

The nature of "nothingness," on the other hand, is not toxic. We live immersed in emptiness. The emptiness

110

in our stomachs, which is satisfied and therefore goes away; the emptiness in our lungs, which expand and contract; the emptiness of our minds, which makes our creativity possible...the emptiness that lets us occupy and vacate, be and not be. Emptiness is a measure, and as such, it is real.

Insatiability is suffocating because it is not by nature a measure. It is merely the relationship between a measure and what this measure might be. And everything "that might be" is not real. Our mental construct of what might be is a model, but it isn't part of reality. And reality is the only dimension where we can find wellbeing. If we look for experiences outside reality, the result will be the unwelcome feeling we usually call "sadness." Being sad means living a life dissociated from desire and reality. "More" is a construct because it's not our body that generates this demand; it comes from our human imagination. Against the screen of our imagination, we process a multitude of fascinating scenarios and projects, but this is also where sadness is bred. If we were to liken the human being to the world, its imagination would be Hollywood, the place that movies come from: epic films, romances, comedies. But for every act of imagination, there comes the moment when the lights are turned back on and we have to get out of our chairs. The movie's over.

"More" is a movie—a movie that replaces the reality expressed in "emptiness." "More" is a ploy for experiencing "emptiness" without ever giving up "having." Desire suggests that we listen to our beloved knocking at the door; desire is the source of the question "to have or not to have" (to be or not to be). This is what the Creator allowed Adam and Eve: desire. The Creator dangled a fruit in front of them, offering it so they would not taste of it. Would this be a sadistic or a romantic Creator? Would He be an incoherent Creator or an Artisan endowing his creatures with characteristics that would enable them to transcend the limits of their own nature?

We can understand Adam and Eve and the terror they felt before the divine offer of being made in the image and likeness of their Creator. Art is by definition empathetic; the key feature of an artist's work is that it is imbued with the artist himself—in other words, the artist shares his nature with whatever he creates. What every true artist wants is not merely to create works he dominates or controls. His gift is to share aspects of his own essence with his creation. A creature who is also capable of creating and enjoying his own independence is the true creation, the object of art. After all, the true Creator does not seek to have but maintains an erotic relationship with the emptiness of having or not having. How much to have of his own work and how much to not have is what ensures possession. And possession is the greatest motivation—as always, possession not of the other but of one's self.

The result, however—that is, the shadow cast within the human being—is the paradox of being both creature and creator. Because of this paradox, we try to fill the emptiness of our earthly situation with "matter." Adam and Eve will turn their backs on possession and insist instead on having. They will renounce the independence tendered by their Creator, represented by the doubt between having and not having; they will trade it for the false relief of having once and for all.

Adam and Eve invent the civilization of "more." Repeated by every generation, their action is to rush to the door even before their beloved knocks. As king of the evolutionary chain and the gardener responsible for this planet, the human being avoids the risk of opening the door too late. In our human prudence, we cannot bear the thought that our beloved might no longer be at the door. Better to risk getting there too soon, because we think it's better to rush in than be a fool. So we become the civilization of "more," the civilization of people who seek to have instead of grappling with the doubts, ambivalences, and paradoxes of having or not having.

In our mental construct or imagined model, we fashion a safer scenario. Yet at the same time, we have brought upon ourselves feelings of insatiability and sorrow.

Our greatest salvation lies not in possessing things but in our very desire. It may seem impossible or utopian to envision a civilization that doesn't want to have and yet does not succumb to the depression of not wanting to have. We feel this kind of scenario would only be

113

possible if human nature were to change drastically, something that seems quite unlikely; yet the economics of our desire works towards this. If we don't know how to manage this "emptiness" that is so filled with possession and life, we will become intoxicated by a world crammed with things that don't bestow existence upon us but instead depersonalize us and transform us into one more thing. From creatures in a work of art, we transform ourselves into just another piece of art, a copy, an imitation made from the repetition of other things. And a clone is not a true creature; we find neither art nor creation in it.

Managing the economics of desire is your most sacred task. This means maximizing your imagination without getting lost in it. Maximizing "emptiness" without missing out on opportunities and maximizing "not having" without forfeiting possessions are also facets of our ongoing balancing act in life. In short, desire is a measure. A little bit more or a little bit less, and the measure of our desire is no longer accurate. Our happiness is directly tied to this accuracy. Too much or too little, and we won't be happy; managing our existence means tweaking the proportions until we get them just right.

In addition to being a measure that demands our attention to its accuracy, desire is also by nature a feeling and not a thought. The basic difference is that feelings, unlike thoughts, do not lie. Our perception of someone else's feelings may be mistaken, but we are never mistaken about our own. This is the link between feelings and reality—they are not illusions. In fact, we should rely on our feelings and constantly embrace them as a therapeutic method for wiping away our sorrows. As mentioned earlier, sadness is a by-product of lies and being out of touch with reality. Only feelings can bring us back to reality, where desire comes from.

Feelings want possession, and thoughts want to have. Since our thoughts can tell lies through our imagination, they will always tell us it is good economics to have. If thought is given a choice, it will invariably opt to have. Thanks to its ability to investigate and to build models, thought will always prefer to have things under its dominion and monopoly. But thought is imprecise. It doesn't know life, and it bases its economics on the samples and patterns it detects, not on reality per se. If thought sought the advice of feelings, feelings would never let it be sidetracked. But thought fears feelings, because feelings are entangled with the Evil Impulse, and thought believes it is constantly responsible for curbing this impulse.

What really confuses us is that the Evil Impulse is a wild card. By the rules of the game, it can move about between feelings and thought. It is a child's feelings that want "mine to be mine and yours to be mine." We have seen how it is thought that teaches us to postpone gratification and control our wish for immediate satisfaction by turning to values. So the Evil Impulse apparently lies within our most primitive feelings and not within our thoughts. But now it is clear to us that the Evil Impulse can also disguise itself in the form of thought. Like feelings, it doesn't want to open the door to the beloved, reveling instead in the seductive tension stirred by prolonged waiting. Desire must remain in this place of tension; if you attempt to capture or control it, it will become a fetish and when you least expect it, your beloved is no longer at the door. Desire disappears. On the other hand, thought rushes to the door, wanting to have the beloved right away. It thinks the sooner it has her, the more guaranteed its possession. But possession lies in the relation between the hand that knocks at the door and the heart that hears this sound.

The human paradox is that we lie neither in our feelings nor in our thoughts. So where are we to be found? Where is the subject of my self?

In the sphere of this complex economics, the most telling variables do not come from the outer world but from the inner. The changes and fluctuations inherent to "being", make set parameters infeasible. There is no set "being" that faces the question "to have or not to have." Being is defined through this relationship. The subject is the one who desires and takes possession; both are relationships and not essences. There is no *a priori* "I" without the world. There is no way of being without having or not having.

I POSSESS, THEREFORE I AM — *FUI ERGO SUM*

From another angle, existence means recognizing that being lies more in queries, ambivalences, doubts, and paradoxes than in an entity—in an "I" that only finds an absolute subject in the Artist. With its borrowed image and likeness, the piece of art does not see itself in its own light but in the light refracted in the world. "To have or not to have" is the vision of ourselves, which momentarily forms an "I" that expresses desire and is capable of taking possession.

This is actually the *self* with which I gradually identify. Of course we are not talking about a static "I" that can state "I am." Nor is this a mutating "I" that I know through my biography. The self is the "I" that is paying attention to these changes; it is the "I" that exists in queries, ambivalences, doubts, and paradoxes. My awareness of the interactions that give rise to such questions is the "I" which keeps me company throughout existence. The way in which this consciousness enlightens and colors reality accounts for the self, for the only location from which I can experience wellbeing and happiness.

Having is a distortion that attempts to use the outer world to produce a static or mutating "I" but one where I am not. There is only someone within me when I pose these queries, ambivalences, doubts, and paradoxes

117

about the world. In the void between having and not having, between the knock on the door and answering it, there lies my presence.

In other words, possession is the essential question. Whoever is in this world lives in search of possessions. For human beings, possessions meet not only physical but also emotional, intellectual, and spiritual needs. The man who possesses is the man who is. How tragic the search for self in a world filled with so many articles, with so many things that are had but that were not submitted to the existential test of "having or not having."

Because we have these things but not the legitimacy gained by asking questions about "having or not having," it would be wise if we were to engage in an age-old technique employed by many mystics. The mystics used begging as a vital spiritual practice at certain moments of their lives. When they realized they were confused and living at a remove from their own lives, they would resort to this artifice. Confusion rooted in the spiritual realm can only be undone by working through it at very concrete levels. To this end, the mystics left the spiritual realm and moved into the mental realm, which is characterized by doubt. From there they dove even deeper into concrete realms, reaching the sphere of emotions and their ambivalences, where feelings never ever lie; at most, they may be mistaken, but their legitimacy and honesty cannot be called into question. Then the mystics made their final pilgrimage, into the physical world, where they grappled with their physical questions, with "things," and with matter. This is why they became beggars.

By losing everything and no longer having, they were able to rebuild their world of possessions. Their goal was to rid themselves of the residue and impurities of things that had not been subjected to the rigors of having or not having. In the world of having, a beggar is what a baby is in the world of being. Begging serves as a reincarnation, a quest to become different by reviewing relationships with what one has.

Yet most of us are terrified of doing something like this and forfeiting what we have. We feel we will lose our essence along with our "things." Without what I have, I am not I. And with this false identity, we wander sadly through life. We so often find ourselves feeling jealous as well, believing that others are living our life—the life we lack the courage to embrace. We think that he or she who possesses this or that is precisely the "I" who I am not and who others have expropriated.

When we do not depend upon "things" in order to be, then there is no envy. Because then we don't want to have anything someone else might have; what we want to have are our own queries, doubts, ambivalences, and paradoxes. While having may seem transferable and impersonal, on the other hand, having or not having represents a unique, non-transferable experience. For in fact we are no longer dealing with having but with possession.

I want to emphasize that not all the "questions" we're talking about are automatically expressions of "emptiness." In an effort to fill in this emptiness, we resort to complicated tricks, often creating identical words for concepts with totally different meanings. Rather than delineating the boundaries of the term "emptiness," we often use the very word "doubt" as if it meant emptiness, in the hopes of filling it.

When we are in grave doubt or when we can't decide what attitude to take (usually involving "to have or not to have"), we transform it into a fallacious doubt. We appear to be facing "emptiness," honoring the time between hearing the knock at the door and going to answer it. But this isn't what is really happening. We are resorting to indecision or doubt precisely to avoid the issue of having or not having. These doubts sadden us deeply. When we manage to rid ourselves of them, we feel immense relief.

The doubts I am talking about do not sadden us. Much to the contrary, they kindle yearnings and ripen into desires. But it's quite common for us to have doubts in an effort to avoid having true doubts and addressing their implications.

There is no way to be without having. This interdependence derives from the fact that there is no being independent of the way in which he relates to what he has. Likewise, there's nothing someone can truly have unless his being expresses a desire for possession. Forever intertwined with whatever lends itself to possession, the human being will never manage to escape the ground, dust, and matter that lends him substance—but which does not represent the totality of his being. This image and likeness to the Artisan is the Creator within the creature, the artist within the piece of art.

Being is less personal to my own self than I would like. For the experience that represents my "I" is not a concrete entity but rather its relationship with everything else around it. Being is also more relational than death makes me realize. Death is primarily perceived as something individual and personal, which distorts our perception of everything else that has to do with life. But many sages also say death is not personal. We are deader for others than for ourselves. So death is more an experience of the living—of others—than our own. The only death we experience is the death of others. For an individual, death is perhaps the absolute reencounter with an emptiness that is neither a hollow manifestation nor a vacuum devoid of possessions. Perhaps we are swallowed up by the same emptiness that fuels desires, by a nothingness that is very full, by the presence that exists between knocking on the door and answering it—an invisible presence but one that rescues us from our status as a piece of artwork and reunites us as part of the artist. In other words, what is everlasting is the art inside us.

I ONLY WANT WHAT I HAVE

True possession can only occur in a paradoxical fashion. Both the lover who neither rushes to the door nor lags behind and the space between the questions elicited by having or not having represent a tense, empty place where we can better grasp a sense of being. Opening doors too soon or ignoring the knocking of our beloved, attaching ourselves to having or feeling aversion towards not having—any of these options distorts our sense of self and jeopardizes our quality of life.

This is the hardest lesson of all.

The Rabbi of Berditchev once saw a man hurrying down the street. He approached him and asked: "Why are you in such a rush?" "Sir, I'm after my livelihood!" the man answered in a huff. "But how do you know," the rabbi went on, "that your livelihood is running ahead of you? Perhaps it's behind you and all you need to do is to stand still…but you are always running away from it!"

We consider it a given that we can only take advantage of opportunities if we pursue them, but often the way we find them is by standing still, detached from the impulse to have and to conquer. It's obvious that life involves effort and seeking, but this same life also affords us grace. That which comes gratis and makes us grateful represents an important part of what can be possessed. What comes for free is inherently tied to the not having that we must constantly take into account along with having. If we don't take the possibility of not having into account, we will miss all opportunities for what comes gratis in this world. And whoever engages solely in the struggle to have will unlikely gain possession of the things that run behind him. So desire is transfigured in this person who dashes madly about the streets.

Perhaps the experience that most closely mirrors this paradox is time. The more we do, the faster time passes, and we end up doing less and less. It is only when we do little that time drags by, allowing us to accomplish a lot.

We run into this paradox whenever we try to live in the extremes, avoiding questions and their implications. It is not a question of having nor of not having, there can only be possession in the tension between having and not having.

Another rabbi, Rebbe Pinchas, said: "Whatever you pursue avidly, you will fail to obtain. But whatever you allow to grow slowly, respecting its time, this you will obtain." Possession is always squatter's rights to our self; it is the legitimate taking possession of one's self and not of things, contrary to what we insist on believing. This is why everything that grows slowly lends itself to possession, while whatever we strain to hold onto proves fleeting and rare.

Those who mechanically try to apply this teaching often find themselves lost in their desire. "To have or not to have" is not a trick, but a true portal through which we can constantly enter the experience of being alive. We can only experience this through deep integrity, by shunning manipulations, tricks, or shortcuts. It is told that a man complained to his spiritual mentor: "I learned that those who *don't* pursue fame and honor are the ones who will truly find them. And this is what I've done my entire life, but the teaching was not born out. I have achieved neither fame nor honor." The rabbi was quick to explain: "That's because even though you weren't running after fame and recognition, you were always peeking to see if they were coming after you, and that's the same as running after them!"

This possession of self that we've talked about so much is only made possible through our questionings. Our ambivalences, doubts, and paradoxes produce the experience of existence. Things do not grant us existence; desire does. The things we can have are only the objects of our desire. But what desire wants is not things; desire wants us to keep on experiencing desire.

Our quest to balance these tensions, which are the natural habitat of desire, is in itself the task of existence. The possibility that we may "have" can tauten the cord of life and draw a harmonious, melodic existence from it; but it can also let out so much slack that our existence grows out of tune and out of step.

Rabbi Susya used to say: "I only want what I have!" With these words, his intent was to disquiet us, planting the idea that our desire should not be attached to something we have yet to get or haven't achieved. He was trying to stress that desire is not the quest for "more" but for emptiness. The things he had and those he still wanted were certainly not detached from the question of having or not having. Desire will always arise from the tension between having and not having. What Susya refused to accept was the illusion that the beloved knocking at our door is Desire. Desire doesn't need his beloved; he only needs her to knock. This is why he doesn't need "more"; he is satisfied with the emptiness that resounds in his heart when he hears the knock. This thumping on the door may become synchronized with the thumping of our own hearts, letting us desire what we already have or, as an ultimate possession, to have nothing more than what is already available to us.

We discover that this knocking suffices and our hearts awaken to honor our responsibility to be, independent of any need to monopolize or own our beloved—this itself constitutes true possession. What I have and what I want is myself. And this is the great gift of existence: if true possession is always of ourselves, as long as we are alive, as long as we are embodied in ourselves, possession is always possible.

"I only want what I already have!" means I only want myself. The object of my desire is to take possession of myself; that is, what I want is by definition what I already have. This is not about narcissism but about recognizing the total reversibility between being and having—being is having one's self. And where does this having come from? It comes from everything in the universe that I may seek to have or not to have and that will bring me back to possession of my self.

Along this path fraught with traps and illusions, where optical illusions confuse the outer world with the inner, the "I" with the other, and the individual with everything around him, our heart is nevertheless awake. It is only this heart that can awaken us from fantasies and from numbness. Only this heart can tear us away from the fetish of our imaginations and fatuous routines, rescuing us so we can hear the knocking at the door. It is not a hallucination of our desire to have but the constant possibility of taking possession—of taking possession of our selves, caressing our doubts, ambivalences, and paradoxes. With this caress we try to probe the invisible and capture the edges of emptiness—and by caring for ourselves in this way, we fulfill our task of being.

THE ULTIMATE CONSUMPTION: OUR SELVES!

Throughout these pages, I have repeated that the object of true possession is the appropriation of our selves. An individual's essence dwells in an absolutely precise place that should not produce either guilt or regret. Guilt is a ghost; it measures how far we have wandered from this precise place because we have more than we can appropriate. Regret measures how far we have wandered because we have less than what we can appropriate. Both measurements illustrate how hard it is to live our own lives and to consume the potential offered up to us during the course of our existence.

This center of human existence is determined by the intersection of the four components of experience: physical, emotional, intellectual, spiritual. When we manage these four areas of our sensitivity in balanced fashion—when the intellectual does not repress the physical, when the physical does not numb the emotional, when the spiritual does not disqualify the intellectual, when the emotional does not disguise the physical, and so on—then the act of possession takes place. This is possession of self, which is possible at every moment of our lives. Because we are a body, we can have it at any time. But we can only have it when we achieve harmony between our sensitivities—we can only have it if we are. At the top of our consumer's wish

127

list is the wish to consume ourselves. Spending and using ourselves is what the economics of a living being is all about. Neither the miser nor the spendthrift of his existence knows possession of self. Taking care of ourselves is the way we can appropriate our being and take hold of the only legitimate subject that can possibly be inside a living entity.

The mystics pondered a worm and concluded that when it comes to existence, it makes no sense to think in terms of a hierarchy in the chain of evolution. As unsophisticated as a worm is compared to a complex human being, the worm can still make itself a worm better than man can make himself a man. This fulfillment of self is as legitimate as its capacity to produce wellbeing, irrespective of any biological hierarchy. Fulfilling one's self and appropriating one's self determines the quality of being.

Wellbeing has nothing to do with the existence of favorable external conditions but with our interactions between our inner and outer selves, between all the kinds of questions we manage to generate.

The Brazilian poet and philosopher Raul Seixas— lying somewhere between Shakespeare and Kafka— puts it plainly: "I am the beginning, the end, and the means." My consciousness makes me into the subject that takes me from birth to death, from the beginning to the end. My consciousness assumes the journey between a tight fist and an open hand, between attachment and detachment. This consciousness is constructed by the emotional and intellectual realms. But, more importantly, I am also the means. Existence courses through me; I don't cross it as if I were walking through a biography. This means is the physical and the spiritual. These are the dimensions that are real only in the present, and they determine the course by which we exist.

While in the middle of my course, I am represented neither by a tightly closed fist nor an open hand. In the middle lies only the question of taking or casting aside, having or not having.

I am the means. I am not life in birth and I am not death in dying. I am what I possess, what I have and have not, and the one who has profound questions and dwells within them.

Through these questions, I acquired an "I" and I recognize a "You."

Habitual companions, these questions ensure that my being lies more in the means than at the beginning or the end. They ensure that occupying my self affords me possession like nothing else in the universe can. I leave the body of a child who believes its soul lies within whatever it desires, and I embody desire itself.

And my wakeful heart reminds me: someone's knocking at the door!